COWGIRLS
IN THE
KITCHEN

RECIPES, TALES, AND TIPS FOR A HOME ON THE RANGE

JILL CHARLOTTE STANFORD & ROBIN BETTY JOHNSON

TwoDot®
Helena, Montana
Guilford, Connecticut

A · TWODOT® · BOOK
An imprint and registered trademark of Rowman & Littlefield

Distributed by NATIONAL BOOK NETWORK

British Library Cataloguing-in-Publication Information Available

Library of Congress Cataloging-in-Publication Data Available

ISBN 978-1-4930-2408-7 (paperback)
ISBN 978-1-4930-2409-4 (e-book)

♾™ The paper used in this publication meets the minimum requirements of American National Standard for Information Sciences—Permanence of Paper for Printed Library Materials, ANSI/NISO Z39.48-1992.

It just seems right that I rededicate this new cookbook—a blend of *The Cowgirls Cookbook* and *Keep Cookin' Cowgirl*, plus lots of new pictures and recipes from my co-cowgirl in the kitchen, sister Robin—to the two women who started me on this journey over twenty-five years ago on a pack trip up the Minam River to the Eagle Cap in the Wallowas of Eastern Oregon following our trip to the Pendleton Round-Up. That was the start of all the books, all the friends I have made because of the books, the enjoyment of the research of the old-time cowgirls, and an entirely new chapter in my life. So—Joanna Stewart and Joan Triplett—this is for you, cowgirls, again.

With love,
Jill Charlotte Stanford

And for me, it just seems absolutely right to dedicate my part of this cookbook to my sister and co-author, Jill. It is such an honor that she asked me to share this culinary adventure with her. Yes, we have had many adventures in the kitchen together over the years, and I know that we will in the future, but this was extra special and I have loved every minute of our collaboration. She is the real cowgirl after all in my eyes, and I am the happy sidekick going down this trail together.

Robin Betty Johnson

COWGIRLS AT THE TRIANGLE RANCH RODEO

CONTENTS

ACKNOWLEDGMENTS

I could not have done this alone.

So I want to thank, with loud ringing and clanging of the dinner bell, the following people:

Erin Turner—my long-time editor and a real cowgirl at heart.

Robin Johnson—who not only cooked for five months and took pictures of what she cooked, she had good suggestions for new recipes and changes on some of the old ones, making this book a real "revision."

Charmain Murray—who galloped right up with offers to help. She gallantly cooked and photographed everything I sent to her and made good suggestions as well. Well done, cowgirl!

Coi E. Drummond-Gehrig, Digital Image Collection Administrator, Denver Public Library, is my go-to person at the Denver Public Library. Coi sends me the suggestions for the historic photos in all my books, and her choices are always dead-on. It is always a pleasure to work with her.

All my friends—here in Sisters and on Facebook—your support and encouragement meant a great deal to me. A special tip of the hat to Susan Bee Kernan-Windell and Kathy Davidson Wolfe. This was a fun project—all the tasters had a ball sampling and criticizing and making awfully good suggestions.

Robin L. Green—who supplied the whip and spur when I needed it, as well as two perfect pictures. Our evening in The Dalles with The Barrel Racer was very special.

FROM THE COLLECTION OF JILL CHARLOTTE STANFORD

JUST GOOD GRUB

Every cowgirl knows the word grub, an inelegant word that means "the food of the West." Eats, vittles, edibles, meals, provisions, rations, eatables, and chow are other words for the plain cooking that makes up the backbone of ranch life among others. It's been said that cowgirls season with three ingredients: salt, pepper, and catsup. And it's almost true! There are no "bouquets garnis" in Cowgirl cooking, nor will you hear the word chiffonade or croquette bandied about in these recipes. Should you ever talk to a cowgirl or a rancher about her cooking, you would not want to use a word like cuisine. Just put the word grub to work, as in, "That was some good grub (or eats or vittles) you rustled up for us tonight!"

On a cattle drive, grub was simple but hot and filling, served up around the chuck wagon to the hungry, hardworking cowboys who ate their meals right out of a tin plate while sitting on the ground. The camp cook (called simply "cookie"—because no one had time to remember their names, and they often didn't stay for more than a season of cattle drives because the job was difficult) had to come up with three meals a day, cooked over an open fire, in all sorts of weather. Many of the things that we eat today, and take for granted, were standard fare from the chuck wagon—coffee you can stand your spoon up in; biscuits made in an iron frying pan; soups and stews in the kettle over the fire; beef, of course; and perhaps some type of fruit cobbler for dessert, but only if there was fruit available (dried apples were a staple in the chuck wagon supplies). Food left on the plate was an insult to the cook. The women who cooked three meals a day in log cabins, "soddys," or hastily built farmhouses wallpapered with old newspapers for insulation were not all that different from the camp cooks. They had to cook everything—usually three meals a day for family and hired help—on a wood stove, or before the wood stove arrived in the back of a wagon, a wood fire outside. They had to grind the coffee beans—no Keurigs. The food had to be fresh, as there was no refrigeration, except in the worst of winter when things could be stashed out in the snow, or pickled and "put up." Nearly all of the food prepared and consumed was homegrown.

The trip to the nearest town that had a general store was often long and arduous. Staples were bought infrequently: coffee beans, flour, sugar, salt, lard, and lye for making soap. Everything was grown or raised and butchered.

We do not apologize for the ingredients you will find here in this new book. Yes, there are a few "cream of" soups, prepared mixes, and tubes of biscuits. Many of the cooks who contributed these recipes live far, far out and away from a handy grocery store in case they run out of something. They know and appreciate the convenience of prepared mixes and cans, to say nothing of the shelf life. It's what they do with these things that makes these recipes special.

Way out West in Idaho

Slow cookery is a big part of this book. Like the pioneer women who put everything in the iron kettle and buried it in the coals of a fire outside or hung it over the fire in the cabin and let it stew all day, you can load up your trusty slow cooker and go do other things.

The biggest addition to this book is the hiring on of another camp cook, my sister, Robin Betty Johnson. Her expertise and knowledge, and her willingness to stop using the words *garnishes* and *Bon Appetit*, and begin thinking about cowgirl cooking, has been a great experience for both of us. She is an imaginative cook and came up with some wonderful and delicious things! Photography could be her next calling. She might even buy a pair of cowboy boots after this experience, testing and creating the type of food so loved by cowgirls for this book. We really were two cowgirls in our kitchens and here are the results.

We have said it before, and we will say it again: Always trust a cowgirl. Cowgirls shoot straight and never lie. They whip up a delicious meal at a gallop, and they make it look easy, because it is. That is the point of these recipes. They are simple and satisfying, just like Cookie would want them to be. If you complimented a dish, he (or she) would dig his (or her) worn-leather boot toe in the dust and say, blushing, "Aw, it's just good grub!"

Jill Charlotte Stanford
Sisters, Oregon

STARTERS AND SNACKS

PUNCHY "FRIED" PICKLES

My sister, Cowgirl Robin, came up with this wonderful variation on fried pickles. These are out of this world! Served with a mug of cold beer, it just does not get any better on a sultry afternoon when the chores are done. Yes, there are two breading mixtures to deal with, but trust me—it's worth the little bit of extra effort.

For the dipping sauce
1/4 cup mayonnaise
1/4 cup sour cream
1/2 teaspoon Worchestershire sauce
1/4–1/2 teaspoon Cajun seasoning (more if you like it hot)
2 tablespoons catsup
1 teaspoon horseradish sauce (more if you like it horsey!)

For the "fried" pickles
1 16-ounce jar of round-cut pickles with ridges (either dill or bread and butter)

For the egg mixture
1 large egg
1/4 cup whole milk or heavy cream
3 tablespoons flour
1/2 teaspoon Worchestershire sauce
1/2 teaspoon seasoned salt

1. Make the dipping sauce so it is cold when you're ready to dip. Mix all the dipping sauce ingredients together and put in a small serving dish in the refrigerator.

2. Drain the pickles and lay them out individually on a large cookie sheet that has been lined with paper towels. Place more paper towels on top and blot them well. Set aside.

ROBIN JOHNSON

3. Preheat the oven to 450°F. Line one large or two medium baking sheets with parchment paper.

4. Prepare the egg and breading mixtures. For the egg mixture, whisk all ingredients together until well combined and frothy. For the dry breading mixture, put all ingredients in a medium bowl and stir to combine well.

5. Dip the pickles, one at a time, in the egg mixture and then in the dry breading mixture. Lay the breaded pickles on the parchment-lined baking sheets. Then, for a thicker crust, dip every pickle in each mixture again before baking (optional, but delicious).

6. Place the cookie sheets in the oven and bake for 8 to 10 minutes, then turn the pickles over, and bake another 5 minutes, until golden brown.

Best served hot and straight out of the oven with the sauce.

SERVES 4

For the dry breading mixture
1 cup bread crumbs
1/4 cup fine yellow corn meal
1/4 cup grated Parmesan cheese
1/2 teaspoon granulated garlic
1 teaspoon Cajun spice mix
1/2 teaspoon paprika (any kind)

It ain't braggin' if you can do it.

—Dizzy Dean

COWGIRL'S CAVIAR

This recipe is often called "Cowboy's Caviar." You can be the judge of whether it tastes better with the new name.

4 cups peeled and diced
   tomatoes
1 medium sweet onion, diced
1 green bell pepper, seeded
   and diced
1 (16-ounce) bag frozen corn,
   thawed and drained
1 (16-ounce) can black-eyed
   peas, drained
1½ cups Italian dressing
1 tablespoon chopped
   cilantro
Sour cream

1. Combine all ingredients well in a blender. Mix on low and for not very long.

2. Put the mixture into an attractive bowl and garnish with a dollop (or two) of sour cream.

3. Serve with tortilla chips and your favorite drink. Put your feet up and enjoy the sunset.

SERVES 4

Your horse is a mirror to your soul. Sometimes you might not like what you see . . . sometimes you will.

—Buck Brannaman

HEN'S ARMS

These wonderfully named morsels are simple, quick, cheap, and good. Our thanks to Shirley Dotten of Parkdale, Oregon, for serving them to us and giving us the recipe. Shirley raises and trains llamas—not horses—for packing in the mountains. Her knowledge of packing, knots, ropes, and gear is breathtaking.

1. Preheat oven to 325°F.

2. In a skillet, heat the oil and fry the wings until golden. (Tuck the end part of the wings under the other two parts to "fold them up.") Drain the wings and put them in a Dutch oven or casserole dish.

3. Combine the honey, catsup, and vinegar (and soy sauce if desired). Pour this mixture over the chicken wings, cover, and bake for 30 minutes.

MAKES APPROXIMATELY 18 WINGS

4 tablespoons vegetable oil
2 pounds chicken wings
1 cup honey
1/2 cup catsup
1/2 cup cider vinegar
2 tablespoons soy sauce, or to taste (optional)

JILL STANFORD

HOLIDAY CHEESE BALL

Asked to a holiday gathering? Asked to bring something? Tired of dips? This is what you bring to the party! You will be asked for the recipe! Ho Ho Ho!

½ cup pecans or walnuts
8 ounces cream cheese at
    room temperature
5 ounces crumbled blue
    cheese (or 3 ounces blue
    cheese and 2 ounces sharp
    cheddar cheese)
½ teaspoon garlic salt
½ teaspoon paprika
½ cup chopped dried
    cranberries
Salt and pepper to taste

1. Preheat the oven to 350°F.

2. Arrange the nuts on a cookie sheet in one layer and toast for 8 minutes. Take them out, let them cool, and then chop them fine. Place in a small bowl or dish and set aside.

3. Combine the remaining ingredients with a mixer and then, with wet hands, form the mix into a ball and let it chill, covered, in the refrigerator for 30 minutes to an hour.

4. Take mixture out of the refrigerator and roll it in the toasted nuts until it is well coated. Serve with crackers.

MAKES 1 CHEESE BALL

ROBIN JOHNSON

CURRIED BITS AND BRIDLES

This was a staple at our parents' gatherings. Our mother and her friend Mary Louise took an old stand-by recipe and made it their own. Thank heaven they wrote it on a recipe card. As little kids we thought it was the best thing ever. Which to eat first? The rice thing? The wheat thing? A pretzel? So many choices! Mix up a bowl of this old favorite and watch it disappear. Spicy and sweet, it will be a crowd-pleaser.

1. Preheat the oven to 250°F.

2. Melt the butter slowly and then stir in the seasoned salt, Worcestershire sauce, granulated garlic, curry powder, cinnamon, and cayenne. Set aside to cool.

3. In a large bowl, mix Rice Chex, Corn Chex, Cheerios or Wheat Chex, nuts, and pretzels together.

ROBIN JOHNSON

4. Pour a third of the butter mixture on the cereal mix and stir. Repeat two more times until the cereal mix is covered.

5. Spread the cereal mixture evenly over a large rimmed baking sheet or a 9 x 13-inch baking dish. Bake in the oven for 1 hour. Stir the mixture often. If you use a 9 x 13-inch baking dish, spread the hot mix on a large sheet of parchment or wax paper or on a cookie sheet to cool.

6. Take a taste. Not salty enough for you? Sprinkle a little Kosher salt on the mix and keep tasting until it is the way you like it!

MAKES 8 CUPS

8 tablespoons butter
1½ teaspoons seasoned salt
1½ tablespoons Worcestershire sauce
½ teaspoon granulated garlic
¾ teaspoon curry powder
½ teaspoon cinnamon powder
¼ teaspoon cayenne powder
2 cups Rice Chex
2 cups Corn Chex
2 cups Cheerios or Wheat Chex
1 cup salted mixed nuts (or salted peanuts if you prefer—not dry roast)
1 cup pretzels (square or bow shaped)
Kosher salt to taste

PATTY'S SHRIMP

True story. When we were guests at a working cattle ranch in eastern Oregon, we offered to help out in the kitchen. We thought something to eat before dinner would be nice while the cowboys had a beer or iced tea. We had noticed that "Cookie" had a bottle of vermouth (it was pretty dusty) in the pantry, and we knew just what to fix. After going to the store (which was thirty miles away) for most of the ingredients, we prepared an appetizer for the evening meal. The cowboys were not too sure about it until they had some. They liked it. We got a postcard from Cookie a week or so later, asking for the recipe for "Patty's Shrimp." He said, "The boys have been asking for it again."

So we wrote out the recipe for Shrimp Pâté and sent it back to the Rural Route. We expect they are still enjoying it.

1 pound cooked shrimp meat
1 pound cream cheese
½ teaspoon dill weed
1 teaspoon Dijon mustard
3 green onions, finely chopped
2 tablespoons chopped parsley
1 teaspoon lemon juice
Dash of dry vermouth or to taste

1. Lightly chop up the shrimp, then add all the other ingredients and mix well.

2. Put the mixture into a serving bowl and refrigerate until you are ready to serve it with crackers. PS: We did not get fancy on the boys—we bought Ritz.

SERVES 6 APPRECIATIVE RANCH HANDS

JILL STANFORD

RANCHY POPCORN

Friday night. Chores are done. Football game is on. Hungry for a snack? This will do it! (Go Hawks!)

1. Mix the ranch dressing mix with the brown sugar, paprika, and chili powder blend; set aside.

2. Pop the popcorn in the microwave according to package directions.

3. When popped, pour popcorn in a large bowl and toss with the spice/sugar mix.

SERVES 3–4

1/2 packet dry ranch dressing mix
1 teaspoon brown sugar
1 teaspoon sweet paprika
1/2 teaspoon chili powder blend
1 bag microwave popcorn

ROBIN JOHNSON

MCKENZIE RIVER KITCHEN GRANOLA

Need a quick pick-me-up snack? A good way to start your day? A gift of something homemade? Robin has developed this delicious granola. I tasted all her attempts until this one was the winner! We think you will agree.

½ cup pecans, slightly chopped

½ cup almonds, slightly chopped

½ cup sweetened and flaked coconut

5 cups old-fashioned oatmeal, uncooked

¼ cup coconut oil (canola oil is fine as a substitute)

¼ cup sunflower seeds

Grated zest from 1 orange

¼ teaspoon salt

¼ cup real maple syrup

½ cup honey

½ cup dried currants

¼ cup dried cranberries

¼ cup dried apricots, cut into slivers

1. Preheat the oven to 325°F.

2. Combine chopped nuts, coconut, and oatmeal in a large bowl; set aside.

3. Combine the oil, sunflower seeds, orange zest, salt, syrup, and honey in a small saucepan and warm over low heat. Stir until everything is combined.

4. Pour the heated liquid into the oatmeal mixture and stir until the mixture is completely covered. Spread the mixture evenly over a large rimmed baking sheet (or two medium ones).

5. Place baking sheet(s) on the middle rack of the oven. Bake for 45 minutes, checking often and stirring occasionally. When mixture is golden brown, take it out of the oven, stir in the dried fruit, and allow to cool.

6. Store mixture in airtight containers (plastic bags also work) and enjoy for several weeks. It also freezes well.

MAKES 8 CUPS

ROBIN JOHNSON

COWGIRL SUMMER SAUSAGE

When the leaves begin to turn and the snow appears on the high peaks, it's time to make summer sausage from the venison you have prepared. This is so good by itself or with cheese and crackers.

1. In a large bowl, mix all the ingredients with your hands as if making meat loaf.

2. Cover the bowl and refrigerate for 24 hours.

3. Take the meat mixture out and knead one more time. Then make 4 (approximately 14 x 2-inch) logs. *Note:* When rolling the logs into shape, make sure you knead the meat and form a tight log so no cracks form during baking.

4. Put the logs on a cookie sheet that has 1- to 2-inch sides (to catch the fat) and bake at 300°F for 3 hours.

5. Take the logs out of the oven, let them cool enough to handle, and then wrap each, first in wax paper, then in aluminum foil. Place in the refrigerator until well chilled.

6. Serve by slicing and eating alone or with crackers and cheese.

MAKES 4 SAUSAGE LOGS

3 pounds ground venison, plus 2 pounds ground beef*
5 tablespoons liquid smoke (found near barbecue sauces)
5 tablespoons Morton Tender Quick (found in a dark blue bag in the spice aisle)
2 tablespoons coarse ground pepper
2 tablespoons minced garlic
2 tablespoons mustard seeds

*IF YOU DIDN'T BAG A DEER, THEN MAKE THIS WITH 5 POUNDS OF GROUND HAMBURGER, BUT DO NOT USE LEAN HAMBURGER.

GARDEN ZUCCHINI FRITTERS

Anyone who has ever grown a garden anywhere in the United States has made the mistake of planting one too many zucchini. This leads to the old jokes about people in small towns locking their cars during the height of summer to keep from coming back and finding a backseat full of zucchini. Or finding a large zucchini in their mailbox, unwanted and unasked for. Well! Try this recipe and you'll be going door-to-door asking, "Any spare zucchini?"

1 pound zucchini, or 1 large zucchini
Salt
1 green onion, chopped (stems, or green part, only)
½ teaspoon minced jalapeño
1 teaspoon cumin seed
2 tablespoons all-purpose flour
1 egg, beaten
¼ cup olive oil
Greek-style yogurt for garnish

1. Shred the zucchini and put it in a colander. Sprinkle generously with salt and mix well; set aside, in the sink, to drain, about 30 minutes.

2. Rinse the shredded zucchini under cold water. Pick up a small handful, squeeze it dry, then place in a clean kitchen towel. When you have squeezed all the zucchini, gather up the towel and twist it to wring out any excess liquid.

3. Put the zucchini in a bowl and add the green onion, jalapeño, and cumin. Stir in the flour, then the beaten egg. The mix will be sticky. If there is still some liquid, add a little more flour.

4. Pour the olive oil into a nonstick skillet. Heat the oil until it is hot enough to make a piece of zucchini sizzle.

5. Drop 4 mounds (2 to 3 tablespoons each) of the zucchini mixture into the skillet, flattening them a little with the back of a spoon. Fry until golden brown, about 3 to 4 minutes. Flip over and fry 2 to 3 minutes more.

6. Remove to a paper towel and pat away excess oil. Serve immediately with a dollop (heaping tablespoon) of thick Greek-style yogurt.

SERVES 4

The Wild Bunch!

"CLARA BELCHER" "LAURETTA BUTLER" "BONNIE McCARROL" "RUTH ROACH" "FOX HASTINGS" "TAD L..." "PEARL GIST" "DONNA COHAN"

O'NEILL PHOTO CO.

The Wild Bunch DENVER PUBLIC LIBRARY

This photograph from the 1920s depicts some of the best-known and beloved rodeo cowgirls in the business. Many of them are particular favorites of ours! Let's examine their outfits. From the left: Clara Belcher, for a long time the only rodeo cowgirl who did bulldogging, is wearing leather chaps with her initials on them and some pretty fancy inlay work. Next to her is Lauretta Butler, who rode saddle broncs, wearing satin pantaloons with a matching top. Bonnie McCarroll, who excelled in saddle bronc riding, is also wearing a satin shirt and plain leather "shotgun" chaps. Ruth Roach, who loved saddle bronc riding and was an All-Around Champion several times, looks pretty proud of her "woolies," chaps made from angora fleece. Fox Hastings was one of the first female bulldoggers in rodeo history. Her fastest time was seventeen seconds, a record she set in 1924. Her leather chaps have pockets and concha embellishments on the side. Tad Lucas is next to Fox and is wearing woolies as well. Tad was a trick rider, but would not have worn these while performing. Pearl Gist was a trick roper, and she's in jodhpurs. Last of all is Donna Cohan, also wearing jodhpurs and a fancy satin sash. It might be a safe bet that the ones in the jodhpurs are in or are about to be in a relay race. All of these intrepid women are wearing the biggest ten-gallon hats they can muster, and nearly all of them are wearing a silk scarf around the neck, known as a "wild rag."

SALOON MEATBALLS

 Out West, saloons always offered their patrons something to eat, like pickled eggs. The idea was that if patrons had something in their stomachs, they wouldn't get as tipsy. If you are having a gathering in your own private saloon, I highly recommend these. Quick and easy to do!

½ cup catsup
½ cup brown sugar
¼ cup any good whiskey
1 teaspoon fresh lemon juice
1 teaspoon Worcestershire sauce
1 (1-pound) bag frozen meatballs, or 18–29 meatballs (needs to be frozen, precooked meatballs)

1. In a medium bowl, combine all the ingredients except the meatballs.

2. Place the frozen meatballs in a Crock-Pot and pour the whiskey sauce on top. Mix so each meatball is coated with sauce.

3. Turn up the heat to high. Leave it on high for about 1 hour, stirring a couple of times.

4. Once the meatballs have thawed, turn the Crock-Pot down to low. The meatballs are ready to serve—either straight from the Crock-Pot or you can transfer them to a deep dish. Alternatively, you can cook, and serve, the meatballs in a deep skillet placed on a trivet or hot pad to protect your table. Put a shot glass of toothpicks next to the serving piece and provide napkins.

SERVES 4

COWGIRL COFFEES, COCKTAILS, AND OTHER DRINKABLES

HOMEMADE CARAMEL CREAMER

This is so simple, and you won't have to pay the high price at the grocery store. Better yet? You can make it taste the way you like by adding more vanilla, less vanilla—you get the idea.

1½ cups sugar
½ cup water
1 cup heavy whipping cream
1 teaspoon vanilla
4 cups half and half

1. Mix the sugar and water in a saucepan; bring to 240°F. Remove the pan from the heat.

2. Using a whisk, slowly add the cream and vanilla to the sugar water. Then add the half-and-half and whisk well.

3. Allow the creamer to cool completely before pouring it into a quart jar. Store in the refrigerator.

MAKES 6 CUPS

JILL STANFORD

COWGIRLS CARAMEL CIDER

Fall is one of our favorite times of the year. Time to pull out the cozy sweaters, wild rags, warm hats, and gloves. It can get real nippy at night, and a hot beverage seems to be in order. This is a great "First Fire of Fall" drink!

1. Mix the apple cider, cinnamon, and brown sugar in a large pot. Heat over medium-low heat, stirring occasionally, until liquid just begins to steam. Then slowly add the vodka. Turn off the burner.

2. While the cider keeps warm, rim four mugs (or glasses) with the brown sugar by dipping the rims in warm water and then "swirl" them in the brown sugar. (We like to add a little coarse salt in this rimming sugar.)

3. Pour the warm cider into the rimmed glasses and serve.

SERVES 4

4 cups apple cider
1 tablespoon cinnamon
1/4 cup brown sugar
1 cup caramel vodka
1/2 cup brown sugar in a saucer
2 tablespoons coarse salt (optional)

JILL STANFORD

COWGIRL'S TEA

This recipe, sometimes called Russian Tea, has been around for a very long time. It was first served to us by Adrianne Brockman. She rode hunters and jumpers, showed a beautiful black Arabian horse in a variety of Western classes, and was the only woman on the Lake Oswego Hunt Club Polo Team. She was a real cowgirl!

You can adjust the ingredients to your own personal tastes. I know one cowgirl who puts cinnamon candy (about a quarter cup) into the mix. "Spices it up," she says. You can divide the mixture into smaller mason jars, tie a bit of raffia around the lid, and give as a winter gift.

2 cups powdered Tang
1 cup powdered instant tea
1 cup sweetened lemonade
   mix
1 teaspoon ground cloves
1 teaspoon ground cinnamon
2 cups sugar

1. Combine all the ingredients in a large bowl and mix well. Put the mixture into a large jar and seal tightly.

2. To serve, put 2 teaspoons (or more) of the mix into a cup and add boiling water. You can put a drop or two of whiskey in your cup if it's been a long day.

MAKES 40 SERVINGS

Aim at a high mark, and you will hit it.

—Annie Oakley, 1860–1926

HORSE'S NECK

A Horse's Neck is a cocktail made with bourbon (or brandy) and ginger ale, served in an old-fashioned or highball (8-ounce) glass with a long spiral of lemon peel (zest) draped over the edge of the glass. It looks very much like a tired old nag's neck.

Dating back to the 1890s, the drink started out as a nonalcoholic mixture of ginger ale, ice, and lemon peel. By the 1910s, bourbon or brandy was added for a "Horse's Neck with a Kick."

1. Pour the bourbon or brandy and ginger ale over ice in an 8-ounce old-fashioned or highball glass. Add the bitters if desired and stir gently.

2. Drape the lemon peel over the rim of the glass, leaving the "neck" hanging out over the edge.

MAKES 1 COCKTAIL

2 ounces bourbon or brandy
8 ounces ginger ale
2–3 dashes Angostura bitters (optional)
1 long spiral of lemon peel for garnish

JILL STANFORD

LAVENDER BLOSSOM COCKTAIL

Sometimes, a cowgirl wants something kinda "girlie." This ought to do the trick.

Shaved ice
1 jigger (1½ ounces) gin
Dash of Lavender Simple
    Syrup (recipe below)
Splash of sparkling wine
Fresh blueberries or lemon
    peel for garnish

1. Place the ice, gin, and Lavender Simple Syrup (in that order) into a tall bar glass. Stir gently with a long-handled spoon; top with a sparkling wine finish.

2. Add a few fresh blueberries or a lemon peel cut into a fine strip for garnish.

JILL STANFORD

Lavender Simple Syrup
1 cup sugar
1 cup water
¼ cup fresh or dried lavender
    blossoms

1. In a medium saucepan, combine the sugar and water. Bring to a boil, stirring, until sugar has dissolved.

2. Add the lavender blossoms. Allow to cool. Strain to remove the blossoms.

3. Store syrup in the refrigerator in a glass container. This is also refreshing in lemonade.

MAKES 1 COCKTAIL

MEXICAN COFFEE

Here is an eye-opening way to greet the dawn, south-of-the-border style! Especially good and warming if you are north of the border—way north and it's snowing.

Mexican coffee is traditionally served in a clay cup along with a pastry. Might we suggest one (or two) Better-Than-the-Bakery Bacon Maple Bars, found on page 44.

1. Pour freshly made, strong coffee into a mug or cup, then stir in the sugar to taste.

2. Add the cinnamon, a little at a time, stirring well.

3. Put a generous amount of whipped cream on top, then sprinkle with a little more cinnamon.

SERVES 1

12 ounces brewed (bold) strong coffee
1–2 tablespoons brown sugar, to taste
1 teaspoon cinnamon
1–2 tablespoons whipped cream

JILL STANFORD

RANCH HOUSE MILKSHAKE

A very simple recipe for a vanilla milkshake. When you add chocolate syrup, you have a chocolate milkshake. Fresh berries or fresh peaches in the summer are wonderful, and crushed peppermint candies during the holidays make this milkshake quite festive. Just try not to spill the milk.

2 cups vanilla ice cream
1 cup 2% milk
2 teaspoons vanilla extract

1. Put all the ingredients into a blender, then add your favorite flavors if you like.

2. Blend on high for 1 minute.

3. Pour into tall glasses, get your straw, and go out on the porch.

MAKES 2 MILKSHAKES

The real things haven't changed. It is still best to be honest and truthful; to make the most of what we have; to be happy with simple pleasures; and to be cheerful and have courage when things go wrong.

—Laura Ingalls Wilder

RODEO 'RITA

In 1910 the first Pendleton Round-Up was touted as "a frontier exhibition of picturesque pastimes, Indian and military spectacles, cowboy racing and bronco busting for the championship of the Northwest." It turned out to be that and more. "The largest crowd in Pendleton's history," seven thousand strong, showed up for the first show on September 29, 1910. Today Round-Up remains a strong tradition.

After a hard day in the chutes, here's a cocktail "double damn guaranteed" to cure what ails you. Made from a blended Canadian whiskey, the 80-proof oak barrel-aged whiskey uses glacier-fed spring water from Mount Hood, Oregon. It's widely known as "the Cowboy Whiskey." We would add it's a favorite among cowgirls, too.

1. Pour salt into a shallow saucer. Run a lime wedge around the rim of an 8-ounce highball glass, then dip it into the salt in the saucer.

2. Pour the Pendleton Whisky and margarita mix into a cocktail shaker filled with crushed ice. Shake and serve over ice in the prepared highball glass.

3. Garnish with a lime wedge, and "Let 'er buck!"

MAKES 1 COCKTAIL

1 teaspoon salt
2 lime wedges
1 ounce Pendleton Whisky
3 ounces margarita mix

THE BARREL RACER

I've said it before and I'll say it again: Pendleton Whisky is "the" choice of cowgirls every-where. To prove it, here is a recipe (joke alert) "making the rounds." Photographer and friend Robin Green and I thought it was so good, we kitchen tested it twice. No, make that three times . . . then we lost track of how many.

2 ounces whiskey (Pendleton preferred, but your favorite will do)

Strong iced coffee, sweetened and with milk or cream added

1 package mini powdered donuts

1. Pour 2 ounces of Pendleton Whisky (or the whiskey of your choice) into a short highball glass.

2. Add ice, maybe 5 cubes.

3. Add iced coffee.

4. Grasp a mini-donut with your fingers. Dip the donut into the coffee/ whisky mixture and take a bite of the soaked part of the donut. Repeat. You should finish it in three bites—turn and burn, baby! Repeat. My best time was way under 17.5 seconds. Robin was right up there with me. We are plan-ning another go-'round.

MAKES 1 COCKTAIL

JILL STANFORD

Alice Greenough Orr—Born to Be a Cowgirl

"We came from a great era. We called ourselves the 'Wild Bunch.'" —Alice Greenough Orr

Alice Greenough Orr was born March 17, 1902, the daughter of a rancher near Red Lodge, Montana. She started breaking colts early and had a talent for staying on no matter how much they bucked. When she was fourteen, she left school and started delivering mail on horseback. The route was thirty-five miles long, and often deep snow hampered her progress.

Her interest in bronc riding (as well as trick riding) started in 1929, and she became an internationally known rodeo performer, performing in forty-six states as well as in Australia and Europe. She had tea with the queen of England. She was inducted into the National Cowboy and Western Heritage Museum in Oklahoma City, Oklahoma; the National Cowgirl Museum and Hall of Fame in Fort Worth, Texas; and in 2010 the Montana Cowboy Hall of Fame in Wolf Point, Montana. She is considered "hands down the first rodeo queen."

A sidenote to Alice's story is that her sister, Marge Greenough, along with brothers Bill and "Turk," were all involved with rodeo and film stunt work. "The Riding Greenoughs" were very popular with their many fans. Alice died in 1995 at the age of ninety-three at her home in Arizona.

Alice Greenough Orr DENVER PUBLIC LIBRARY

WATERMELON ICE

It can get awfully hot and dusty in the corrals during branding and roundup time. This thirst-quencher was served in tin cups during a lunch break at a roundup outside of Ontario, Oregon. Jill was lucky enough to be asked to help and trailered her horse, Tune, four hundred miles just to be a part of a vanishing way of life. She is still not certain just how much help she was—Tune was no help at all—but the cowboys were patient and kind and saw to it that she didn't get into too much trouble. She came back with this cooling and refreshing beverage we have made a summer tradition.

2 cups diced, seeded
  watermelon
1 cup light corn syrup
2 tablespoons lime juice
Tequila (optional)

1. In a large bowl, mash the watermelon until smooth. Add the corn syrup and lime juice. Stir well. Cover and freeze for 2 to 3 hours, until almost firm. Beat with a wooden spoon, then freeze again.

2. Spoon mixture into short 8-ounce glasses and provide spoons. You can add 1 jigger of tequila per serving for an extra "kick."

MAKES ABOUT 4 CUPS

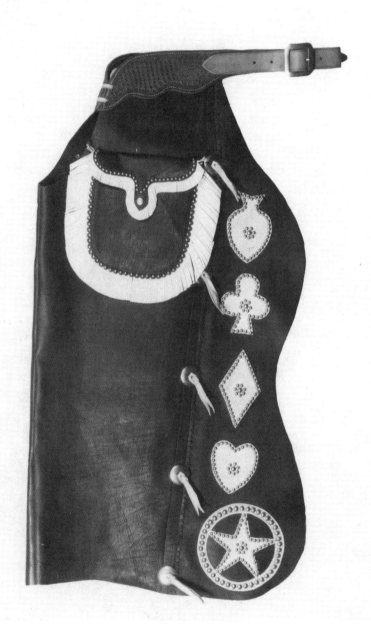

BREAKFASTS AND BRUNCHES

ALL-AMERICAN STEAK AND EGGS

This is a truly hearty breakfast, but also remember that "breakfast for dinner" can be a wonderful way to end the day. This recipe is simple and easy.

1 tablespoon vegetable oil
1 pound sirloin steak, about
    1-inch thick
Sea salt and black pepper
2 tablespoons butter
8 large eggs

1. Preheat the oven to 350°F.

2. Preheat a large cast-iron skillet over medium heat until hot, about 5 minutes. Raise the heat to high and add the oil.

3. Season the steak generously with salt and pepper. Place the steak in the skillet and cook, turning once, until well-browned, about 4 minutes per side. Transfer the steak from the skillet to an oven-safe platter. Place the steak in the oven and cook for 5 minutes more for medium-rare.

4. Transfer the steak to a cutting board. Cover it loosely with foil and let it rest for 10 minutes before carving. (The reason it's a good idea to let meats rest is so the juices can go back into the meat.)

Turn off the oven and put 4 plates in the oven to warm.

5. While the steak is resting, cook the eggs. Heat two skillets over medium-low heat, placing a tablespoon of butter in each pan. Break 4 eggs into each skillet. Season the eggs lightly with salt and pepper, and cook until the whites are just set, about 3½ minutes. (If you want the yolks to be cooked through, cover and continue cooking for 1 to 2 minutes more.) Divide the eggs onto the 4 plates you've warmed in the oven.

6. Cut the steak on a diagonal into thick slices, divide the slices among the 4 plates, and serve immediately. You might want some thick slices of buttered toast to sop up the egg yolks. Just sayin' . . .

SERVES 4

Didn't anyone tell this cowboy it is bad luck to put your hat on the bed? But maybe he already has bad luck. That horse shoe nailed to the wall is upside down, letting all the luck run out!

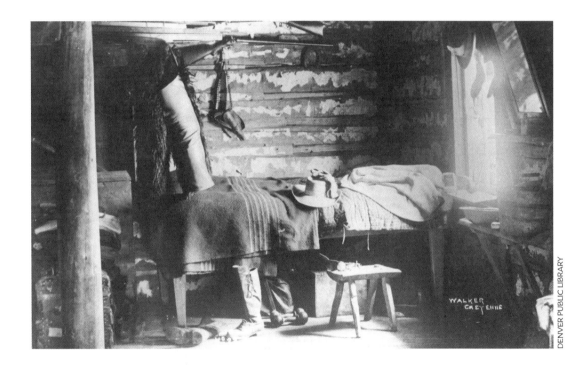

BREAKFAST APPLES

A hearty breakfast is the only way to start the day out West. This easy-to-do apple dish is good on its own, but it's even better on top of oatmeal with a little cream. This dish is guaranteed to help you get through the branding until lunch! You can also serve this over ice cream (see page 176 for a nifty, quick way to make ice cream) back at the ranch house for dessert.

3 tablespoons butter

3 medium tart apples, peeled, cored, quartered, and sliced

⅓ cup sugar, plus 2–3 tablespoons

1. Melt the butter in a cast-iron skillet over medium heat.

2. Add the apples to the skillet. Cover and cook for 5 minutes, or until the apples are juicy and browned. (If you are cooking these over a campfire, use aluminum foil for the cover.)

3. Turn the apples and sprinkle with the ⅓ cup of sugar. Reduce the heat to low (or move the skillet on the grill of the campfire away from direct heat). Cover again and cook for about 5 minutes longer. Uncover and cook 2 to 3 minutes longer, or until the sugar is absorbed and the apples are lightly browned on the bottom.

4. Remove apples from the heat and sprinkle with remaining sugar. Best served warm.

Note: Save the apple peels and cores for the horses.

SERVES 6

ROBIN JOHNSON

BURNIN' DAYLIGHT OATMEAL

 "Sun's up! Strike a trot! We're burnin' daylight!" That's the traditional call of the foreman to his hands before they head out onto the range to gather cattle. On a cold and miserable morning, modern-day Cowgirls might want to serve this wonderful oatmeal devised by Robin.

1. Make the old-fashioned oats as directed on the package for the amount you want. This recipe calls for 1 cup of oats added to boiling salted water. Cook on medium-low for 5 minutes. Put a lid on the cooked oatmeal and let it rest for about 5 minutes.

2. Divide the cooked oats between 2 or 3 bowls. Sprinkle with the apples or pears (or a mixture of both), walnuts or pecans, sunflower seeds, coconut flakes, and dried fruit. Pour some warmed milk into each bowl, and top with either brown sugar or maple syrup to taste.

You can put everything into your slow cooker that has been sprayed with nonstick spray. Put the lid on, set the temperature to low, and cook for about 7 hours.

SERVES 2-3

1 cup old-fashioned oats
1¾ cups water or milk
Pinch of salt
½ cup cut-up apples or pears
¼ cup chopped walnuts or pecans
⅛ cup toasted sunflower seeds
2 tablespoons toasted coconut flakes
2 tablespoons each golden raisins, cut-up dried figs, apricots, and dates
1 cup warmed milk
Brown sugar or maple syrup to taste

JILL STANFORD

SLOW COOKER CHRISTMAS CASSEROLE

 On Christmas morning the kitchen will be filled with the wonderful fragrance of this breakfast dish that has been quietly "doing its thing" while you dream of sugar plums or a pony. Thanks to cowgirl Charmain Murray for the idea!

1 32-ounce package frozen potatoes O'Brien, divided

½ pound bacon, cooked, cooled, and broken into pieces

1 package breakfast sausage links, browned, cooled, and sliced

½ cup diced green pepper

½ cup diced red pepper

½ cup chopped fine sweet onion

2½ cups shredded cheddar cheese, divided

10 eggs

1 cup whole milk

½ teaspoon dry mustard

Salt and pepper to taste

Sour cream and/or salsa for serving

1. Spray the inside of a slow cooker generously with nonstick spray.

2. Layer the potatoes, bacon, sausage, peppers, and onions in two or three alternating layers.

3. Spread the cheese on top.

4. Beat together the eggs, milk, and mustard, adding the salt and pepper at the end.

Pour this mixture over the potato mixture in the slow cooker.

5. Cover and cook on low for 6 to 8 hours, or until the eggs are set and cooked through.

6. Let the casserole cool down, with the lid still on, for 15 minutes.

Top each serving with a dollop of sour cream. Cowgirl Susan likes salsa on top (We've got one on page 165).

SERVES 6-8

CINNAMON ROLL PANCAKES

We are pretty sure you have a box of biscuit baking mix in your pantry. We know we do! These are a great change for those mornings when pancakes are just what you want for breakfast.

1. In a large bowl, whisk together 2 cups of the biscuit baking mix, 1 cup of milk, and the eggs until smooth. Set aside.

2. Preheat a griddle to medium heat. In a small bowl, combine the melted butter, brown sugar, 1/4 cup biscuit baking mix, 1 tablespoon milk, cinnamon, and vanilla. Whisk together until smooth. Add a teaspoon more milk if needed to make the cinnamon mixture thin enough for piping. Transfer the mixture to a large plastic bag and snip a small corner from the bag for piping.

3. Spray the hot griddle with nonstick baking spray. Transfer 1/3 cup of batter to the griddle. Immediately pipe a swirl of cinnamon around the pancake to make it look like a cinnamon roll. Then spray a thin layer of nonstick spray right over the top of the pancake. When it's ready to flip, flip it and cook on the other side until golden. Repeat until all the batter and cinnamon mixture is gone. Serve with your favorite maple syrup.

MAKES ABOUT 24 SMALL PANCAKES

2¼ cups biscuit baking mix, divided
1 cup milk, plus 1 tablespoon
2 large eggs
¼ cup butter, melted
⅔ cup loosely packed brown sugar
3 tablespoons ground cinnamon
1 teaspoon vanilla

DUTCH FUNNEL CAKES

Here is a timeless—not to mention swirly and pretty—breakfast dish that is a lot of fun to make! Did we say delish as well? Kids and grownups enjoy this old-fashioned breakfast fried cake. Sprinkle it with powdered sugar, a sugar/cinnamon mixture, or melted butter and maple syrup. Any way you choose to do it, this is a surefire winner!

You will need a funnel for this recipe, or we used a large measuring cup with a pointed spot.

2 cups canola oil
3 eggs
2 cups milk
1/4 cup sugar
3 1/2 cups flour
1/2 teaspoon salt
2 teaspoons baking powder

1. Preheat the oil in a straight-sided and deep skillet over medium-high heat (if using an electric frying pan, preheat to 375°F). Leave room between the oil and the top of the pan to allow room for batter to be added.

2. Beat the eggs in a medium bowl; add the milk and sugar. Beat well.

3. In a separate bowl, sift the flour, salt, and baking powder. Add to egg mixture. Beat until batter is smooth. Batter should be thin enough to flow through the opening of a funnel. If needed, add a little more milk.

4. Put your finger over the bottom of the funnel and pour batter in the top.

5. Remove your finger and drizzle the batter into the hot oil, making criss-crosses and swirls. Let the cakes brown on the bottom and then carefully flip them over with tongs to brown on the other side.

6. Place the cake on a paper towel to drain for a minute. "Garnish" to taste.

MAKES ABOUT 8 CAKES

HANDY BREAKFAST

This ingenious recipe came to us by way of a ranch wife living out in Northern Idaho. She says, "With a toddler to feed, a husband to make breakfast for, and often as not, a puppy or a kitten to take care of in the kitchen, I find this lets me eat with one hand and tend to the rest with the other one."

16 slices bacon
1 (16.3-ounce) tube
    refrigerated buttermilk
    biscuits
8 eggs
Salt and pepper to taste

1. Preheat the oven to 350°F.

2. In a 10-inch skillet, cook the bacon over medium heat about 4 minutes, or until cooked but not crisp, turning once. (It will continue to cook in the oven.) Drain and set aside on a paper towel.

3. Spray 8 (6-ounce) muffin cups or 8 (6-ounce) glass custard cups with cooking spray. Separate the dough into 8 biscuits. Place a biscuit in each muffin cup, pressing the dough three quarters of the way up the sides of the cups. Place 2 bacon slices in each biscuit cup and crack an egg over each. Season with salt and pepper.

4. Bake 25 to 30 minutes, or until egg whites are set. Run a small knife around the cups to loosen. Serve immediately.

SERVES 8

JUNE'S EGGS

A cowgirl will always come to the rescue. When we lamented the fact that we had to serve a buffet-style brunch to a crowd and could not figure out what to do about the eggs, June Lee came to the rescue. This easy-to-make dish, one spiral-sliced ham, a dozen cinnamon rolls, and a bowl of fresh melon balls and we were set!

1. Preheat the oven to 350°F. Spray a 9 x 13-inch baking dish with cooking spray.

2. Beat the eggs in a large bowl. Fold in everything else, and pour the mixture into the prepared baking dish.

3. Bake for 35 minutes, until the eggs are puffed up and browned slightly on top.

SERVES 8

10 eggs
½ cup all-purpose flour
1 teaspoon baking powder
2 cups small-curd cottage cheese
2 cups grated jack cheese
½ cup butter, melted
2 (4-ounce) cans green chiles, seeded and diced

Someday, I'll marry a cowboy.
But first, I want to be one.

—Anonymous

KISS MY GRITS

You do not have to be a Southern belle cowgirl to enjoy grits. Grits are corn—that is ground—period. They can be made in your slow cooker the night before your breakfast. They will be creamy and delicious. Want a bit more of a nudge? They are also low in calories.

1½ cups stone-ground grits
6 cups water
2 teaspoons salt
2 heaping tablespoons sugar
1 cup cream
4 tablespoons butter, plus
   more to taste
Maple syrup or cheddar
   cheese (optional)

1. Spray the inside of a slow cooker with nonstick cooking spray.

2. Add the grits, water, salt, and sugar. Stir well.

3. Cook on low setting for 7 hours or overnight.

JILL STANFORD

4. Before serving, add the cream and butter and stir well. Let the grits "rest" for about 10 minutes before spooning into serving bowls.

5. Serve with maple syrup and a pat of butter. Or top with grated yellow cheese if you are serving the grits as a side dish for supper.

SERVES 8

LIZ'S CRUMMY COFFEE CAKE

If you check out the Walt Disney film Run, Appaloosa, Run!, you will see a girl jumping an Appaloosa horse over a touring car. That girl (who was the stunt rider and stand-in for the star of the movie) is now a woman, cowgirl Elizabeth "Liz" Dixon. She has been riding and jumping throughout her life, and I think she would jump a horse over a car even today. She has real cowgirl spirit, and this is her coffee cake.

1. Preheat the oven to 350°F. Combine brown sugar, flour, spices, and margarine in a medium bowl. With your hands (wash them first after riding, Liz cautions!), crumble all until it is . . . well, crumbly.

2. Remove ½ cup of the crumbles and set aside.

3. To the mixture remaining in the bowl, add sour cream, raisins, and nuts. Stir and blend well.

4. Pour batter into an 8 x 8-inch buttered ovenproof dish. Top with reserved crumbles. Bake for 35–40 minutes until the top is bubbling. Serve warm with strong black coffee.

SERVES 4-6

2⅔ cups brown sugar
4 cups unsifted flour
1 teaspoon cloves
2 teaspoons cinnamon
½ teaspoon salt
2 tablespoons baking soda
1 cup margarine
1 pint sour cream
1 pound raisins
1 cup nuts (walnuts preferred)

BETTER-THAN-THE-BAKERY BACON MAPLE BARS

Cindy Forbes, up in Ronan, Montana, is also known as "Twisty" for her very popular business, Twist N Ties. She makes the most beautiful "wild rags" from silk and other fabrics. Cowgirls can't get enough of these colorful and useful scarves. We have a few ourselves. Not long ago, Cindy posted a recipe for one of our favorite things: Better-Than-the-Bakery Bacon Maple Bars! I asked her about it. She said, "That recipe was super easy. My daughter Robin had made them, so I knew if she could do them, I could too. Actually, hers turned out better than mine! Ha!" So we figured if they could do them, so could we, and so can you.

2 cups canola oil
1 8-count can refrigerated biscuit dough
¼ cup butter
½ cup brown sugar
3 tablespoons milk
1 tablespoon corn syrup
2 teaspoons maple extract (Mapleine)
2–3 cups powdered sugar
4 slices cooked and cooled bacon, crumbled (optional)

1. Pour the canola oil into a medium saucepan and begin heating over medium-low heat.

2. Open the biscuit dough can and separate the 8 pieces of dough. Gently stretch the biscuits into an oblong shape.

3. Make the glaze in a small saucepan by combining the butter and brown sugar. Whisk in the milk and heat for about 5 minutes on medium heat, stirring often, until the butter is melted and the sugar is completely dissolved. Add more sugar, a little bit at a time, until it is the right glazing consistency.

4. Remove the glaze from the heat and stir in the corn syrup and maple extract. Add the powdered sugar, ½ cup at a time, whisking until smooth between additions, until it is thick and not runny. Add 1 to 2 teaspoons more milk, if necessary. The glaze will begin to harden if you leave it sitting—which is what you want! Once all the powdered sugar is added, keep the glaze warm on the stove, whisking occasionally.

5. Now check the temperature of the oil using a meat thermometer; it needs to read 350°F. Increase heat gradually if necessary. Once it is ready, drop the shaped dough into the oil, two at a time. Let them fry and cook for about 2 minutes, then turn and cook an additional 2 minutes. This process of cooking the doughnuts goes very fast, so have a paper towel-covered plate ready to set the bars on when cooked. Bars should be a nice golden brown.

6. Let the bars cool for a few minutes, then whisk the glaze to make sure it's smooth enough to coat each bar. Using a soup spoon (like we did), glaze the top of the bars and allow to cool, glaze side up, on a cooling rack.

7. Repeat this process until all bars are fried and glazed. Carefully add the bacon pieces, if you like, on the glazed top of each maple bar before the glaze sets up.

MAKES 8 BARS

JILL STANFORD

NAPKIN BREAD

Napkin Bread, also called Sticky Bread, Golden Crown, Pinch-Me Bread, or Bubbleloaf, got its name from us because you need several napkins for your sticky fingers. Recipes for the bread first appeared in women's magazines and community cookbooks in the 1950s. Serve it hot so that the baked segments can be easily torn away with the fingers and eaten by hand.

For the bread
½ cup granulated sugar
1 teaspoon cinnamon
1 (16.3-ounce) tube
   refrigerated buttermilk
   biscuits
½ cup chopped pecans
   (optional)
½ cup raisins (optional)
½ cup firmly packed brown
   sugar
½ cup butter or margarine,
   melted

1. Preheat the oven to 350°F. Grease a 12-cup fluted tube pan (also known as a Bundt pan) with butter.

2. In a large plastic bag, mix together the granulated sugar and cinnamon.

JILL STANFORD

3. Separate the dough into 8 biscuits, then cut each biscuit into quarters. Put them in the bag and shake to coat them thoroughly.

4. Arrange the biscuit pieces all around in the pan, adding pecans and raisins (if using) among the pieces.

5. In a small bowl, mix the brown sugar and melted butter. Pour over the biscuit pieces.

6. Bake for 30 minutes, or until golden brown and no longer doughy in the center.

7. Cool in the pan for 10 minutes, then turn upside down onto a serving plate.

8. If using frosting, mix together the powdered sugar and lemon juice with a fork. Then slowly mix in the milk until the frosting has no lumps and will "drizzle" easily. Drizzle the frosting over the rolls.

9. Pull apart the bread to serve—and pass the napkins.

SERVES 4

For the frosting (optional)
1 cup powdered sugar
¼ cup lemon juice
Enough milk to thin the
    frosting to about ¼ cup

MENNONITE BREAKFAST

We got this recipe from a Mennonite lady in Hubbard, Oregon in 1975. She said it was her favorite dish for breakfast when she was growing up. Tangy and sweet, this hot dressing is just the ticket for breakfast, lunch, or dinner. Jill used to quilt with the Mennonite ladies on Tuesdays. She learned a great deal from them, but she never graduated to the "good" quilt on the frame.

4 baking potatoes
4 slices thick-cut bacon
⅓ cup sugar
1 tablespoon all-purpose flour
1 teaspoon Dijon mustard
1 egg
1 cup milk
¼ cup vinegar

1. Preheat the oven to 400°F and bake the potatoes for 1 hour, or until fork-tender. Take them out of the oven and wrap them in a kitchen towel to keep warm while you prepare the dressing.

2. Cook the bacon in a medium pan or skillet over medium-high heat until browned and crispy. Once crispy, transfer to a paper towel-lined plate to drain, but reserve the drippings in the pan.

3. In a small bowl, whisk together the sugar and flour, then stir in the mustard, egg, milk, and vinegar; mix until smooth.

4. Heat the drippings in the pan, then pour in the vinegar mixture. Crumble the bacon into the dressing and cook over medium heat for 5 to 6 minutes, or until the dressing has thickened.

5. Remove from the heat and serve hot over the baked potatoes, which have been split and quartered.

SERVES 4

Note: This dressing is also terrific over salad greens—instant "wilted greens with hot dressing."

RED-EYE GRAVY AND HAM

On a trip to Santa Fe, Jill and her trail partner stopped for the night at a B&B just outside of Durango, Colorado. The woman who ran the place, Betty Nyland, had retired from ranching (by herself) up in the foothills and was tending tenderfoots who passed through. Instead of the usual granola in the morning, she served up a real ranch breakfast. Cholesterol was not in her vocabulary, nor was caffeine. She only knew how to do one thing: Serve up a ranch-style breakfast and serve it well.

1. Heat the butter in a big iron skillet and fry the ham steaks until browned. Add half the water, cover, lower the heat (or move the skillet to a cooler part of the cook fire), and simmer the ham until tender, about 20 minutes. (This was when Betty whipped up the baking-powder biscuits and made a fresh pot of equally strong black coffee.)

2. Take the ham out of the skillet and put it on a warm platter. Scrape the browned bits from the sides and bottom of the skillet and add the remaining water. (There should be about 1 cup in the skillet then.) Stir in the coffee, bring it to a boil. Let it boil a bit to reduce by a quarter or half, until it has thickened some.

3. Pour the coffee mixture over the ham steaks. Serve with hash browns and eggs.

SERVES 4

2 tablespoons butter
4 ham steaks, 1/4-inch thick, or one large bone-in slice
1/3 cup water, divided
1 cup very strong black coffee (last night's pot will do very well)

ROBIN JOHNSON

SAUSAGE GRAVY

Is there anything in this world better than sausage gravy and biscuits? We don't think so!

4 tablespoons butter (Bacon drippings are even better!)
1 pound pork sausage
5 tablespoons all-purpose flour
2 cups whole milk
Salt and pepper to taste

1. Melt the butter (or bacon fat) in a large skillet and then add the sausage.

Cook the sausage over medium heat, breaking it up as it cooks. Continue cooking until the sausage is cooked well, about 8 to 10 minutes.

2. When the sausage is cooked, add the flour and mix well; then let it cook for another 2 or 3 minutes.

3. Add 1 ½ cups of the milk to the skillet and, using a wooden spoon, continue to stir constantly. In a short while it will start to thicken; it is important to continue to stir. If it is too thick, add the remainder of the milk and continue to stir. Eventually it will start to bubble and won't be thickening much anymore. Let it bubble for another 2 or 3 minutes. Add additional milk if it is too thick— you be the judge! Then salt and pepper to taste. Some like lots of pepper in their sausage gravy!

4. Serve over the Buttermilk Honey Biscuits on page "Buttermilk Honey Biscuits" on page 61.

SERVES 4

ROBIN JOHNSON

SOFT SCRAMBLES

Just up the road from us is a woman who sells eggs. Better yet, she sells eggs of beautiful colors from her Araucana hens. (Did you know these chickens are from Chile? We didn't either!) Because the eggs are fresh and delicate, we wanted to find out the best way to treat them so they would stay fresh and delicate. Here is what we learned:

• Fashioning a double boiler from a metal bowl and a pan of gently simmering water creates the low, even heat that eggs love (think custards, curds, and pastry creams).

• Cooking eggs this way yields a scramble with a super-creamy, luscious texture—it takes time, but your patience will be rewarded.

• A rubber spatula helps keep the egg curds from clinging to the bowl, and keeping them constantly moving prevents larger curds from forming for a smoother result.

• You can cook the eggs to your desired consistency; a longer cook time yields tender, fork-friendly eggs, while a softer scramble is perfect spread on hearty toasted bread.

1. Start the water boiling in the pan, then turn the burner to low.

2. In a mixing bowl, beat the eggs and cream together. Season with salt and pepper.

3. Put the butter in the bowl over the simmering water to melt, then pour the egg-cream mixture into the bowl.

4. Cook the eggs over low heat while pushing the eggs around the bowl with a spatula, as if scraping the bowl. Do this the entire time the eggs are cooking. Take the spatula forward and backward and around the pan. Watch the eggs closely—as soon as they reach a creamy consistency, remove from the bowl. Be careful to not overcook. Garnish with parsley.

SERVES 2

3 eggs
1/4 cup heavy cream
Salt and pepper to taste (We like to use lemon pepper.)
3 tablespoons butter
1/2 teaspoon parsley, chopped (or use dried)

JILL STANFORD

CACKLEBERRIES ON TOAST

In certain places in the hills and hollers of Kentucky, eggs are still called cackleberries. Now you know. This is still a good, filling, and simple meal.

3 tablespoons butter
2 tablespoons flour
1 teaspoon salt
2 cups warm milk
6 hard-boiled eggs
Salt and pepper to taste
8 slices toast

1. Melt the butter in a heavy saucepan. Add the flour and salt and stir until well blended.

2. Slowly add the warm milk, stirring constantly, until the sauce thickens. It will still be fairly thin.

3. Separate the egg whites from the yolks. Chop the egg whites and add them to the sauce. Season with salt and pepper.

4. Arrange slices of toast on a platter and pour the sauce over them. Mash the egg yolks through a sieve and sprinkle on top of the sauce.

5. If desired, add a slice of ham before pouring the egg sauce over the toast.

SERVES 8

Some of my best leading men
have been dogs and horses.

—Elizabeth Taylor

FRENCH TOAST CASSEROLE WITH BLUEBERRY AND PEACH COMPOTE

Inside for a Sunday morning or outside on a crisp morning, this dish is sure to please.

1. Generously butter an 8 x 8-inch baking dish and place the bread in the dish.

2. Whisk the next seven ingredients together very well. Pour this evenly on the bread, cover with aluminum foil, and place in the refrigerator overnight.

3. In the morning, bake the casserole at 350°F for 40 to 45 minutes. Uncover half the way through.

4. While the casserole is baking, make the fruit compote to serve on the top. In a small saucepan add the peaches, blueberries, sugar, and water. Bring to a boil and let simmer for about 5 minutes.

SERVES 4

A note from Robin: "The last time I made this (and took the picture) we were camping and didn't have an oven, so I made the custard mix the night before and then cut the bread in slices, dipped them, and fried them on top of the stove in the butter. I then arranged them in a pan and served the compote on top. It was even better with the bacon we served. And all of this out in the woods by a lake in Central Oregon. Jill came for breakfast and said, 'I want this in our book!'"

1/2 to 3/4 loaf sweet bread (like Hawaiian sweet bread) cut into 1- to 2-inch squares
4 large eggs
1 cup whole milk
1/4 cup heavy cream
1/4 cup sugar
1 teaspoon vanilla
1 tablespoon maple syrup
1/2 teaspoon cinnamon (optional)

For the fruit compote
2 fresh peaches, peeled and cut up
1 pint fresh blueberries
3 tablespoons sugar
2 tablespoons water

ROBIN JOHNSON

MAYME STROUD TRICK RIDING BELLE FOUCHE TRI-STATE ROUND-UP.
(A.E.P.CO.INC)

BREADS, BISCUITS, AND QUICK BREADS

ANNIE OATLEY BREAD

Robin found our Great-Aunt Betty Jones's original recipe for this bread. She noticed Betty used lard, and Robin substituted butter. Betty used fresh yeast cakes also, so Robin substituted with dry yeast. Robin notes, "It is her method, hence the overnight rise. This really improves the flavor though, and she knew that. It turned out fine. It is a good, solid no-knead bread."

1 package regular dry yeast
  (not rapid rise)
½ cup, plus 1 teaspoon,
  packed brown sugar
1 cup old-fashioned oatmeal
1 teaspoon salt
½ tablespoon butter
4 cups bread flour

1. Put yeast and 1 teaspoon brown sugar in a small bowl. Pour ¼ cup lukewarm water (about 100°F) on the yeast and sugar and stir to combine. Set aside. It will foam, and this tells you that your yeast is alive and well and starting to work!

2. Bring 2 cups water to a boil. In a large bowl, combine the oatmeal, remaining brown sugar, salt, and butter and then pour the boiling water over the mixture. Stir well until the butter is melted. Cool this mixture over a bowl of cold water until lukewarm (about 100°F).

3. Add the yeast mixture to the oatmeal mixture and then add the flour (about ⅓ at a time), stirring well after each addition. Cover the bowl with plastic wrap and place in the refrigerator overnight.

4. In the morning, unwrap the dough. It will have doubled in size. Stir it down, cover again and let rise on the counter away from any drafts, about 1½ hours, or until double in size again.

5. Oil a loaf pan. Punch or stir the dough down, let it rest for a few minutes, and then put it into the loaf pan. Use lightly wet fingers to shape it into a loaf. Let the dough rise again for about 1 hour, covered with a lightly oiled piece of plastic wrap. (Don't let it rise too far over the loaf pan.)

6. Preheat the oven to 350°F. Bake the loaf for about 40 minutes. The old-fashioned method of testing for doneness is to tap the top. If it sounds hollow, it's done. Cool slightly on a wire rack before turning it out of the pan.

MAKES 1 LOAF

Lady Sharpshooter

Annie Oakley, the famous "Lady Sharpshooter," sent this letter to the then-president of the United States at the onset of the Spanish-American War:

Hon. Wm. McKinley President. Dear Sir, I for one feel confident that your judgement will carry America safely through without war. But in case of such an event, I am ready to place a company of 50 Lady sharpshooters at your disposal. Every one of them will be an American and as they will furnish their own guns and ammunition, will be little if any expense to the government. Very Truly, Annie Oakley

COWGIRL CORN BREAD

A great favorite, both around the campfire or while cozied up in front of a fire, is old-fashioned corn bread. Served with chili or soup, this one—courtesy of Janet Larson, a cowgirl who is at home on the range as well as in front of one in her kitchen near Mitchell, Oregon—is fast and easy and has a few surprises that make it pretty darned special. Just like cowgirls.

1½ cups yellow cornmeal
1 cup whole wheat flour
1 cup unbleached white flour
1 tablespoon baking powder
1 teaspoon baking soda
1 teaspoon salt
2 cups buttermilk or plain yogurt
½ cup milk
¼ cup maple syrup, brown sugar, or honey
2 eggs, beaten
¼ cup butter, melted and cooled

1. Preheat the oven to 350°F. Butter a 9 x 13-inch baking pan or a 2-inch-deep round cast-iron skillet.

2. Sift the dry ingredients into a large bowl.

3. In another bowl, combine all the wet ingredients and stir until mixed.

4. Fold the wet ingredients into the dry ingredients. Smooth the batter into the pan or skillet and bake for 25 to 30 minutes, or until a straw inserted in the center comes out clean. Cool for at least 10 minutes before cutting.

MAKES 12 PIECES

Cowgirls are God's wildest angels. They use cowboy hats for halos and horses for wings. A mane in their face is their Heavenly Grace.

—Unknown

MISS RODEO USA'S PRIZE-WINNING BANANA BREAD

Mackenzie Carr, Miss Rodeo U.S.A. 2012, is beautiful, rides like a champion, is always smiling, is always helpful, and is never anything but a true person. And, she cooks. Her mom, Barb Carr, says, "Mack makes a fabulous banana bread. It's a former Champion Bread from her 4-H days at the Columbia County [Oregon] Fair." We certainly give it a blue ribbon!

1. Preheat the oven to 350°F.

2. Grease two 3½ x 4½ x 2½-inch loaf pans.

3. Cream the shortening and sugar until fluffy. Add the eggs, salt, and baking soda and blend well.

4. Add the bananas and flour, alternating one banana with one cup of flour. Mix thoroughly.

5. Add the buttermilk, vanilla, and molasses and mix again.

6. Pour the batter into the loaf pans. Bake for 1 hour, or until the center is done. Let the loaves cool, then turn out of the pans.

MAKES 2 LOAVES

DID YOU KNOW THAT IF YOU DON'T HAVE TWO EGGS YOU CAN SUBSTITUTE TWO HEAPING TABLESPOONS OF MAYONNAISE? NOW YOU DO!

½ cup shortening
2 cups sugar
2 eggs, slightly beaten
¼ teaspoon salt
1½ teaspoons baking soda
3 "old" bananas, mashed
3 cups all-purpose flour
10 tablespoons buttermilk
1 teaspoon vanilla
1 tablespoon dark molasses

JILL STANFORD

BEER-BATTER BREAD

Simple, fast, and really good toasted!

3 cups self-rising flour
½ teaspoon salt
¼ cup honey
12 ounces any light beer
   (fruit beer is very good)

1. Preheat the oven to 350°F. Grease and flour a loaf pan.

2. Combine the flour, salt, honey, and beer in a medium bowl and stir until just combined.

3. Spoon the batter into the loaf pan. Bake on the middle rack of the oven for 1 hour. The bread is done when a toothpick come out clean, and it has set well in the middle.

MAKES 1 LOAF

ROBIN JOHNSON

BUTTERMILK HONEY BISCUITS

Early in the morning, the smell of biscuits baking in the oven is a promise of a good day ahead. Pour yourself a cup of coffee while they are baking!

1. Preheat the oven to 350°F and lightly grease a baking sheet.

2. Sift the dry ingredients into a large bowl. Cut the shortening in with a fork until it resembles cornmeal. Add the buttermilk and honey and mix well.

3. Roll out the dough to a thickness of 1 inch and then cut out rounds using a glass that you have dipped the rim in flour to keep the dough from sticking. Place the rounds on the lightly greased pan and bake until golden brown.

4. Serve with Easy Strawberry Freezer Jam (page 160) or underneath Sausage Gravy (page 50).

MAKES 16 BISCUITS

2 cups flour
2 teaspoons baking powder
1/2 teaspoon baking soda
1 teaspoon salt
1/4 cup shortening
1 cup buttermilk (powdered will do fine)
1/4 cup honey

Don't screw with me, fellas. This ain't my first time at the rodeo.

—Lulu Parr

BAKING POWDER BUTTER BISCUITS

"Roll out, cowboys!" Many a ranch hand has heard that call early in the morning. Baking powder biscuits (and Sausage Gravy, page 50) are a staple in the cookhouse of ranches all over the West in the morning. Here is a one-bowl, one-pan recipe that will make you feel like going and branding something. Instead of gravy, serve with honey or jam. Or, what the hell, have the gravy!

1 stick (½ cup) butter
2½ cups all-purpose flour
4 teaspoons granulated
    sugar
4 teaspoons baking powder
2 teaspoons salt
1¾ cups buttermilk

1. Preheat the oven to 450°F.

2. In the baking dish that you'll be baking these biscuits in, melt the stick of butter in the microwave. Set aside.

3. In a medium bowl, mix together the flour, sugar, baking powder, and salt. Pour in the buttermilk and stir until a loose dough forms. The batter will be a bit sticky.

4. Using your hands, press the biscuit dough into the baking dish right on top of the melted butter. (If you use wet fingers, the dough won't stick to as easily.) Some of the butter will run over the top of the dough—it will look like a mess, but don't worry.

5. Using a sharp knife, cut the biscuit dough into 9 squares or lines before putting the biscuits in the oven.

6. Bake for about 20 to 25 minutes, rotating the dish once during baking, until the biscuits are golden brown on top. Remove from the oven and let cool before cutting all the way through. Use a spatula to remove the biscuits.

MAKES 9 BISCUITS

ROBIN JOHNSON

CHUCK WAGON DOUGHNUTS

These mouthwatering morsels come from Judy Santille, a woman who was the camp cook for the famed 3X Ranch in Southeastern Oregon for many years. She says that underneath all the bravado, cowboys really like something hot and homemade in the morning before they go out gathering and branding. "These always did the trick," she says.

1. In a large bowl, mix the flour, salt, and baking soda.

2. Add ⅓ cup cooking oil and cut it into the flour mixture with a fork. When it resembles cornmeal, shape the dough into an oval, then with your fist make a "well" in the middle.

3. Pour in the buttermilk and stir until it all comes together. Use your hands if you have to.

4. Flour a flat surface (inside a Dutch oven lid or on a clean, flat rock) and knead the dough 10 or 15 strokes.

5. Heat the remaining oil in a large cast-iron skillet. Pinch off balls of dough, flatten them between your palms, and then drop them into the hot oil. Fry 2 to 3 minutes on each side, or until golden brown.

6. Drain doughnuts on one of the brown paper bags and then drop them into the paper bag filled with the sugar–cinnamon mixture. Shake the bag to thoroughly coat the doughnuts.

MAKES ABOUT 30 DOUGHNUTS

2½ cups all-purpose flour
2 teaspoons salt
1 tablespoon baking soda
2 cups cooking oil, divided
1 cup buttermilk (powdered is okay)
2 brown paper bags—1 filled with 1 cup sugar and 4 tablespoons cinnamon

ROBIN JOHNSON

CINNAMON-SUGAR MUFFINS

1½ cups all-purpose flour
¾ cup sugar
2 teaspoons baking powder
¼ teaspoon salt
¼ teaspoon nutmeg
½ cup milk
1 egg, well beaten
⅓ cup, plus 2 tablespoons butter, melted
½ cup sugar mixed with 1 teaspoon cinnamon

1. Preheat oven to 400°F. In a medium bowl, mix flour, sugar, baking powder, salt, and nutmeg with a wire whisk.

2. In a separate small bowl, combine the milk, egg, and ⅓ cup melted butter.

3. Pour the wet ingredients into the dry ingredients and mix well.

4. Grease muffin tins or use paper liners and fill about two-thirds full. Bake 20 minutes. Brush remaining melted butter over the tops, then sprinkle on the sugar-cinnamon mix.

MAKES 12 MUFFINS

She was unstoppable. Not because she did not have failures or doubts, but because she continued on despite them.

—Beau Taplin

SUMMER BREAD

No one says no to chocolate. Here is the perfect answer to an overabundance of zucchini from your garden, or a well-meaning friend's garden. Some cowgirls frost this with a simple chocolate frosting and serve it as a dessert with ice cream. We like to put cream cheese on a warm slice and serve it for lunch with a simple green salad.

1. Preheat the oven to 375°F. In a large bowl, beat the eggs and then add the sugar. Beat again. Add the oil, applesauce, vanilla, and milk; stir well. Add the zucchini.

2. Sift together the salt, baking soda, baking powder, cocoa, and flour. Add this mixture gradually to the wet ingredients.

3. Pour batter into 2 greased 3½ x 4½ x 2½-inch loaf pans. Bake for 55 minutes. Check with a toothpick for doneness—the tops should be a little bit "cracked." Let the loaves cool before turning out on a wire rack. Like chocolate chip cookies, this bread is best eaten a little warm.

MAKES 2 LOAVES

3 eggs
2 cups sugar
½ cup vegetable oil
½ cup applesauce
3 teaspoons vanilla
½ cup whole milk
2 cups shredded zucchini
1 teaspoon salt
1 teaspoon baking soda
½ teaspoon baking powder
½ cup cocoa
2½ cups all-purpose flour

MAPLE-FLAVORED GINGERBREAD

Cowgirl Charmain Murray asked if she could help out with the task of cooking, eating, and photographing recipes. We gave her this one. She raved about it, and so did her friends. So will you and yours!

2½ cups sifted flour
1½ teaspoons baking soda
1 teaspoon ground cinnamon
1 teaspoon ground ginger
½ teaspoon ground cloves
½ teaspoon salt
½ cup shortening
½ cup sugar
1 egg
½ cup molasses
½ cup maple syrup
1 cup hot water

1. Preheat the oven to 350°F. In a small bowl, sift together the flour, baking soda, cinnamon, ginger, cloves, and salt.

2. In a separate large bowl, cream together the shortening and sugar until light and fluffy. Add the egg and beat well. Gradually beat in the molasses and maple syrup.

3. Add the dry ingredients to the wet alternately with the hot water, beating well after each addition. Pour batter into a lightly buttered 8-inch square baking dish.

4. Bake 40 minutes or until cake tests done by inserting a straw or a toothpick into the center and it comes out clean. Cool in pan on a rack.

SERVES 12

SALADS AND SIDES

GOIN' TO HEAVEN AMBROSIA

You can call this corny—it is. You can call this old-fashioned—it is. This is the "perfect" salad side dish to take to a potluck or serve at the table. Men love it, and cowgirls think it is heaven on a plate. Corny, but heaven nevertheless. We had this in a small Western town, in the Grange Hall, at a potluck and thought it was danged good. Thanks to Luella Parsons for sharing!

1 (8-ounce) can mandarin oranges, drained
1 (8-ounce) can pineapple chunks, drained
1 cup miniature marshmallows
1 cup flaked sweetened coconut
1 cup (8 ounces) sour cream or ready-made whipped cream (This is entirely up to you. A combination, half and half, is good, too.)
½ cup chopped walnuts or pecans (optional)

Mix all the ingredients together well, and refrigerate until well chilled. Some people garnish this with maraschino cherries, which we think is an awfully good idea.

SERVES 6

As a child I always had a fondness for adventure and outdoor exercise and especial fondness for horses which I began to ride at an early age and continued to do so until I became an expert rider being able to ride the most vicious and stubborn of horses, in fact the greater portion of my life in early times was spent in this manner.

—Calamity Jane (Martha Cannary Burke, 1852–1903)

COPPER PENNIES

Way up in Idaho on Fish Hatchery Road, Terry Lane searches out old recipes. She put in a request at Ruralite magazine for a particular pea salad recipe. We sent her a similar recipe, and she sent us this one in return by way of saying, "Thanks." Some of you might recognize the name but don't have the recipe. Now you do. It is a must! This salad goes well with ham for Easter, and it is also a wonderful potluck dish. Sweet and sour, it is a great addition to any gathering.

1. Boil the carrot "pennies" until barely tender. Drain and cool with cold water to stop the cooking.

2. In a saucepan, combine the soup, vinegar, sugar, oil, and salt. Mix well. Heat this mixture until the sugar is dissolved, stirring every once in a while. Add the Worcestershire sauce and mustard and blend well.

JILL STANFORD

2 pounds carrots, peeled and sliced into 1/4-inch rounds (about 2 cups)—these are the "pennies"
1 (10¾-ounce) can tomato soup
3/4 cup vinegar
1/2 cup sugar
1/4 cup salad oil
1/2 teaspoon salt
1 tablespoon prepared yellow mustard
2 teaspoons Worcestershire sauce
1 green pepper, diced
1 medium white onion, diced

3. Put the cooled carrots, pepper, and diced onion in a large bowl and gently mix. Pour the sauce over the vegetables and stir all together.

Allow to the mixture to marinate overnight in the fridge.

SERVES 6

COWGIRL COLESLAW

This is the real deal—coleslaw as it ought to be! It is tart yet sweet, crunchy, and a wonderful side dish to just about everything, especially in the summer for a barbeque.

1/2 cup sour cream

1/4 cup mayonnaise

1/2 cup apple juice (or more to taste)

1 teaspoon dill weed (optional)

Salt and pepper to taste

3 cups thinly shredded cabbage (If you put the shredded cabbage in cold water in the refrigerator for about an hour and then drain well before making the coleslaw, the cabbage will be very crisp.)

2 tablespoons finely diced red onion

1 large tart-sweet apple, peeled and diced. (Some of the best varieties to use are Braeburn, Gala, Gravenstein, Granny Smith, and Jonagold.)

1 carrot, peeled and shredded

1. In a large salad bowl, combine the sour cream, mayonnaise, apple juice, dill weed, and salt and pepper to taste.

2. Mix the cabbage, onion, apple, and carrot into the sauce. Refrigerate for at least 4 hours to allow the ingredients to blend together.

SERVES 6

A Cowgirl's Prayer for You
May your horse
Never stumble,
Your cinch
Never break,
Your belly
Never grumble, and your heart
Never ache.

LEMON LARIAT APPLE RING

This does look like a lariat loop, and it's an old-fashioned and favorite salad.

1. In a large bowl dissolve the gelatin in hot water. Add the lemon juice and chill until mixture begins to thicken.

2. Fold in the diced apples, celery, and nuts.

3. Pour mixture into an 8-inch round salad mold. Chill in the refrigerator until firm.

4. When you are ready to serve this, fill your sink with about 6" of hot water. Dip the filled ring into the water to just the top of the rim. Count to five. Then, remove the ring from the water, put the serving dish on top of the ring and quick as a wink turn it over. The ring will come right out and onto the plate.

5. Combine the mayonnaise and sour cream. Dress the apple ring with the mixture.

SERVES 6–8

2 packages lemon-flavored gelatin
3 cups hot water
6 tablespoons lemon juice
1½ cups diced Red Delicious apples
1 cup diced celery
½ cup coarsely broken walnuts
¼ cup mayonnaise
¼ cup sour cream

SALAD IN A JAR

Jill says, "I seem to have a lot of canning jars, which is odd, because I have never canned a thing in my life. Once I discovered this easy way to take a salad along for a picnic or lunch at work, I have had a lot of fun with it. I use the pint- and quart-size jars. You can make four or five at a time—enough to get you through the entire week without having to painstakingly chop and assemble all of your salad ingredients every day. Wow—what a concept."

1. The dressing of your choice (I like Ranch, of course) goes on the bottom of the mason jar. Use about 2 to 3 tablespoons for a quart-size salad; 1 to 2 tablespoons for pint-size. If you'll be keeping it for longer, consider storing the dressing separately in travel-friendly, 2-ounce container.

2. Vegetables and other things go next, like raw onion (letting these sit in the dressing will mellow them out a bit), bell peppers, carrots, cucumbers, snap peas, grape tomatoes, olives, garbonzo beans, and artichoke hearts. If you're feeling like fruit, grapes and diced apples hold up well—just sprinkle a little lemon juice onto the apples first to keep them from browning.

3. Now you can put some protein on top. Consider chopped hard-boiled eggs, diced chicken breast, ham, canned tuna (drained), or salmon.

4. Time for the greens. Packing the greens tightly will help keep the ingredients in place. Darker varieties pack more nutrients, so skip the iceberg and mix dark greens like kale, spinach or spring mix with chopped romaine.

5. With your mason jar mostly full, now is the time to sprinkle on your favorite toppings. These can be croutons, shredded cheeses, nuts, seeds, and more delicate ingredients like berries and sprouts.

6. When it's time to dig in, turn your jar upside down and pour your salad onto a plate or into a bowl. Or shake things up and enjoy it right from the jar. Don't forget to pack a fork!

SERVES 1

RIO BRAZOS SALAD

1 (15-ounce) can black beans, drained and rinsed
1 (16-ounce) can whole kernel corn, drained and rinsed
1/2 cup seeded and chopped red bell pepper
1/2 cup seeded and chopped green bell pepper
4 scallions, chopped (including the tops), or 1 small Vidalia or Walla Walla sweet onion, chopped
1/4 cup chopped celery
1 (4-ounce) can black olives, chopped
3 tablespoons lemon juice
2 tablespoons tomato salsa, plus more to taste
1 tablespoon olive oil
Salt and pepper to taste
Sour cream

1. In a large bowl, combine beans, corn, peppers, scallions or onions, celery, and olives.

2. In another bowl, stir together lemon juice, salsa, and olive oil.

3. Combine the salsa mixture and bean mixture. Add more salsa and salt and pepper to taste. Refrigerate for at least 1 hour.

4. Top salad with dollops of sour cream.

SERVES 6

Ranch women are as sharp as nails and just as hard. If Eve had been a ranch woman, she would never have tempted Adam with an apple. She would have ordered him to make his meal himself.

—Anthony Trollope, 1862

COWGIRLS IN THE KITCHEN

SHARIE'S SAUERKRAUT SALAD

Sharie Forde of Sisters, Oregon, loves to compete in team penning and sorting—both noisy, not to mention fast-paced, events. She is too modest to say just how many trophy buckles she has won. She says, "The best food is something someone else has cooked." But she does offer this piquant salad, which is wonderful for potluck suppers following a penning or sorting. We think Shari exemplifies this quote by Dale Evans, the "Queen of the Cowgirls": "The Cowgirl faces life head on, lives by her own lights and makes no excuses."

1. Combine all the salad ingredients in a large salad bowl; mix and refrigerate.

2. In another bowl, combine all the dressing ingredients and mix well.

3. Toss the dressing with the salad ingredients just before serving.

SERVES 12-16

For the salad
4 cups sauerkraut, drained
1 (8-ounce) can garbanzo beans
1 cup chopped celery
1 cup shredded carrots
1 small onion, diced
1 (4-ounce) jar pimentos, diced (optional)
1 red or green bell pepper, diced (optional)

For the dressing
1/2 cup vegetable oil
1 cup white sugar
1 cup rice vinegar
1/2 cup poppy seeds
Pepper to taste

THE SALAD

In our families, "The Salad" is the only title or description needed. We all know, instantly, what it is. We have made this every year for Christmas or Thanksgiving dinner since 1969. Now you can, too!

1 (14-ounce) can whole-berry cranberry sauce

3 tablespoons lemon juice

1 cup heavy cream, whipped (If you are pressed for time—and who isn't these days?—you can substitute ready-made whipped cream.)

1 cup broken walnut and pecan meats

¼ cup mayonnaise, plus more for serving

¼ cup powdered sugar

Lettuce leaves, for serving

1. Mix the cranberry sauce and lemon juice together (be careful not to "bruise" the cranberries) and spread the mixture in a 6 x 6-inch glass dish.

2. In a bowl, mix the whipped cream, nuts, mayonnaise, and sugar together, then spread on top of the cranberry mixture.

3. Freeze for at least 3 hours.

4. To serve, let thaw for about 10 minutes, cut into squares, and serve on lettuce leaves. A dollop of mayonnaise is the big finish.

SERVES 6

ROBIN JOHNSON

THE RRR

Here is a very simple and surprisingly good salad. The peppery radishes, the crisp romaine, the subtle ranch . . . heaven.

Put the chopped lettuce and radishes in a bowl. Pour on as much ranch dressing as you want, mix, and serve.

SERVES 4

1 head romaine lettuce, dark outer leaves taken off, chopped
8–10 large radishes, tops and bottoms taken off, diced
Ranch dressing

When things do not go right with you, when the circumstances seem to be against you and Fate deals you a blow between the eyes, remember what the cowboys say in the great Northwest. "Just grit your teeth, get another hold and let 'er buck!"

—The motto of the Pendleton Round-Up, 1911

BACK-AT-THE-RANCH DRESSING

We'll admit it: we love ranch dressing. Why? Because there are so many good things you can do with it. It's good on salad greens, poured over a baked potato, and for dipping crisp veggies and barbeque chicken wings. We like to make our own, and we like to make it simple and basic.

1 cup good buttermilk
¼ cup mayonnaise
3 tablespoons sour cream
2 teaspoons lemon juice
1 medium garlic clove, finely chopped
½ teaspoon sea salt
⅛ teaspoon freshly ground black pepper

1. Put all the ingredients in a 16-ounce mason jar. Close it tight and shake as hard as you can to mix the ingredients. Taste and season with additional salt and pepper as desired.

2. Refrigerate until chilled and the flavors have melded, about 1 hour. The dressing will last up to 3 days in the refrigerator. You can pour it right from the jar—no need for a fancy salad dressing boat.

MAKES 1½ CUPS

A cowgirl gets up early in the morning, decides what she wants to do, and does it.

LILY'S SALAD DRESSING

We met Lily at a horse auction. We struck up a conversation while eyeing a dapple gray mare none of us could afford. We learned that Lily had been a sheepherder in her early years and then settled on a small ranch in central Oregon, where she raised a few fine horses for "everyday work," as she put it. She invited us for lunch and more reminiscing of her days out on the prairies all by herself. Her salad dressing was like nothing we'd ever tasted, and she was pouring it out of a mason jar, over a wedge of iceberg lettuce. We persuaded her to share the recipe.

Put all the ingredients in a quart jar, cover, and shake well. You can add onion (peeled and chopped), 2 tablespoons of dry mustard, or crumbled blue cheese if you want to get really fancy. The dressing keeps well for weeks in the refrigerator.

MAKES 3 CUPS

1 (10.75-ounce) can tomato soup, undiluted
½ soup can vegetable oil
½ soup can white vinegar
Salt, pepper, and sugar to taste

JOLLY GREEN SALAD DRESSING

Instead of ranch dressing, try this recipe.

1 large ripe avocado, diced
2 teaspoons fresh lemon
  juice
½ cup Greek yogurt
1 teaspoon hot sauce
  (optional)
¼ cup extra-virgin olive oil
2 garlic cloves, mashed
¾ teaspoon salt
¾ teaspoon pepper

Put all the ingredients into a medium bowl and mash with a fork. Enjoy over torn-up salad greens.

MAKES ABOUT 1 CUP

FOR EASY, NO-BOIL CORN ON THE COB, TAKE THE HUSK OFF AND PULL THE SILK OFF A FRESH EAR OF CORN. IN A SMALL BOWL, COMBINE 1 TABLESPOON OF MAYONNAISE PER EAR OF CORN, SALT, PEPPER, AND A LITTLE GARLIC SALT AND ONION SALT. RUB THIS MIXTURE ALL OVER THE CORN. THEN SPRINKLE GRATED CHEESE OVER THE CORN. WRAP THE CORN TIGHTLY IN FOIL AND PUT IT ON THE BARBECUE GRILL. TURN ONCE OR TWICE DURING COOKING, ABOUT 15 TO 20 MINUTES. DO NOT TELL YOUR GUESTS HOW YOU MADE THIS STUPENDOUS SWEET AND MOIST CORN ON THE COB.

SANTA FE VEGETABLES

Georgia O'Keeffe has to be considered a cowgirl. She is, after all, an inductee into the National Cowgirl Hall of Fame. Her spirit and style, reflected in her paintings and watercolors done in and around Santa Fe, embody the true West in vivid and dramatic color. We made a pilgrimage to Santa Fe to visit the newly opened Georgia O'Keeffe Museum. There is a vegetarian cafe nearby that serves this wonderful combination of tasty vegetables. O'Keeffe would have loved them and, quite possibly, would have painted them for their riot of colors.

1. Heat oil in a large skillet. Sauté the onion and garlic for about 5 minutes. Add the carrots. Cover the skillet and sauté for an additional 5 minutes, stirring occasionally.

2. Stir in the remaining vegetables and the seasonings and cook on low heat just until the vegetables are tender.

3. Serve open-face on corn bread or in a pita pocket. Top with sour cream.

SERVES 8

2 tablespoons vegetable oil
2 cups chopped onion
2 cloves garlic, minced
3 carrots, cut into half-moons
1 large zucchini, cut into half moons
1 green pepper, seeded and diced
2 cups fresh corn kernels
2 cups chopped and drained fresh, ripe tomatoes
1 teaspoon cumin
1 teaspoon coriander
1 tablespoon chopped cilantro
Salt and pepper to taste
Sour cream, dollop per serving

SUZI'S SOUTHWESTERN RICE

"Get a move on!" is Suzi Hazard's favorite saying. She is up at the crack of dawn and on one of the many horses she trains for clients all over the Southwest. In addition to giving clinics, she likes to cook, but "nuthin' too hard or too special," she says. This fills the bill. "It's even better the next day and, besides, you don't have to cook it the next day," Suzi adds with a twinkle in her eye.

1 (14½-ounce) can stewed tomatoes, undrained
1 (15½-ounce) can black beans, rinsed and drained
1 cup instant brown rice
1 cup canned corn (or fresh, scraped off the cob)
1 tablespoon cumin
½ teaspoon chili powder
Salt and pepper to taste

1. Put everything in a large pan or skillet with a lid that fits tightly.

2. Bring to a boil, reduce heat, and simmer, covered, for about 10 minutes or until the liquid is absorbed.

3. Add salt and pepper to taste.

SERVES 6 HUNGRY RIDERS

ROBIN JOHNSON

BRANDING DAY BAKED POTATOES

 It's going to be a long day in the corrals with the cattle. The steaks are ready to be grilled, and a salad is ready to toss together. Wouldn't baked potatoes be just the thing to have with the steak and salad? You're in luck! Get out the slow cooker and saddle up!

1. Wash and dry the potatoes well. Using a fork, pierce the sides of each potato in several places.

2. Rub potatoes with olive oil and then liberally salt and pepper each one. Wrap potatoes, individually, in generous squares of aluminum foil so they are completely covered and sealed.

3. Place the foil-wrapped potatoes in a slow cooker and cook on high for 3 to 4 hours or on low for 8 hours.

4. Remove the potatoes from the slow cooker and carefully take off the aluminum wrappings. Cut a long slice down each potato and push the ends together to open. Top with butter, sour cream, cheddar cheese, and definitely the bacon!

SERVES 4-6

4-6 medium-size russet baking potatoes
2 tablespoons olive oil
Salt and pepper to taste
1/4 cup butter
1 cup sour cream
3/4 cup cheddar cheese, grated
1/2 cup chopped green onions
1/2 cup cooked bacon bits (optional)

ROBIN JOHNSON

CHEESY GARLIC POTATO CASSEROLE

This is one of Robin's standby dishes. She says it's dangerous to have on hand because you will want to eat it all in one sitting—all by yourself. Double or triple the recipe for big groups—it's a really good thing to take to potlucks!

1½ pounds Yukon Gold
  potatoes
2 tablespoons butter
1 large or 3 small cloves of
  garlic, minced fine
2 tablespoons flour
1½ cups milk
1 cup sharp cheddar cheese,
  shredded
¼ cup Parmesan cheese,
  grated
Salt and pepper to taste
2 tablespoons dry sherry
  (very optional)
Paprika, shredded cheddar,
  and grated Parmesan for
  topping

1. Preheat the oven to 350°F. Butter an 8 x 8-inch or 9 x 9-inch baking dish (or equivalent) and set aside.

2. Wash and peel the potatoes. Cut them into ½-inch cubes (more or less), place in a big pot, and cover with cold, salted water. Bring the water to a boil and cook the potatoes for about 5 minutes. Drain well, put the potatoes in a medium-large bowl, and set aside.

ROBIN JOHNSON

3. In a medium saucepan over medium heat, melt the butter and briefly sauté the garlic in the butter. Add the flour and, stirring constantly, cook for about 3 minutes. Add the milk and continue to stir (using a whisk at this point is a good idea) until mixture becomes thick, about 3 to 5 minutes. Keep stirring and whisking the whole time. Add both cheeses and stir until melted. At this point, if the mixture is too thick, add a little more milk, a little at a time, until it is the way you want it. Salt and pepper to taste. Now you can add the sherry if you want.

4. Fold the cheese mixture into the potatoes and gently combine. Pour or spoon the potatoes into the prepared baking dish, top with toppings, and put in the oven for about 30 minutes. The potatoes will bubble and start to turn golden when done. You can place the dish under the broiler for a few minutes if you want it to brown more—but watch it closely, because it happens fast!

SERVES 4-6

Dead last is greater than did not finish, which trumps did not try!

—Unknown

KENTUCKY CORN PUDDING

Judy Santille has a battered recipe box filled to overflowing with tried-and-true recipes sure to please a crew of cowboys (when she was camp cook for the 3X ranch in Oregon) or guests at her Hotel Diamond table. Most of the recipes are in her head. When it's time for supper, she simply looks into her pantry to see what's on hand and goes to work. In late summer there is nearly always fresh corn. In midwinter canned corn is on the shelves. Either one will do for this hot and tasty dish.

3 tablespoons butter, room temperature
2 tablespoons sugar
2 tablespoons flour
1 teaspoon salt
3 eggs
2 cups fresh, frozen, or canned (drained) corn kernels, coarsely chopped
1½ cups half and half or heavy cream

1. Preheat the oven to 350°F. In a buttered 1½-quart casserole dish, mix the butter, sugar, flour, and salt.

2. Beat in the eggs, and stir in the corn and half and half or cream.

3. Bake for 45 minutes, until slightly puffed and brown.

SERVES 6

A good cook can catch a feller.

JUNE'S RANCH BEANS

June Kintzley Leavitt lives south of Lakeview, Oregon. The sky goes on forever in this remote section of Southeastern Oregon. Pheasant, quail, chukker, grouse, deer, antelope, and elk abound, as do some pretty darned big cattle ranches. June has been the head cowgirl behind the Double Arrow Ranch for many years. Her son John operated Leavitts Western Wear in Sisters, Oregon, for many years. About this recipe June says, "Men really like it. I use it for branding crews and large groups at hunting season."

Combine all ingredients in a big Crock-Pot or slow cooker, cover, and cook on low for about 2 hours. If you'd like some meat, add 1 pound raw ground beef, sausage cut into "moons," or diced leftover ham.

SERVES 10-12

1 (16-ounce) can lima beans
2 (16-ounce) cans kidney beans
2 (16-ounce) cans garbanzo beans
4 (16-ounce) cans pork and beans
3/4 cup brown sugar
1/2 cup vinegar
1 cup tomato juice

Grandpa's Beans

John Leavitt asked me why he wasn't asked to be in this book. We told him it was because he is not a cowgirl. He said, "Then you won't get to know about Grandpa's Beans." We gave in.

"Percy Leavitt was my dad's dad. He ranched outside of Boulder, Utah, the last place in the United States to have the US Mail delivered by pack mule. His recipe is simple: For one person, cut up some bacon, put it in a pot, fry it crisp, then put in one can of pork and beans and lots of pepper. Heat and eat. For two people, two cans of beans and lots of pepper. For three people you get the idea. Just be sure to put in lots of pepper."

109

Photo copyrighted only, 1906 by Morris & Kirby, Chinook, Mont. K 778

A Cow Girl on a Bronco.

Germany.

SOUPS, STEWS, AND CHILIS

BACK AT THE BUNKHOUSE CHILI

Nothing is more satisfying to a tired and cold cowgirl than a bowl of savory stew or soup at the end of a long day gathering and branding. This is where that slow cooker can come in handy! Terry Wilcox sometimes mixes everything in a Crock-Pot and just lets it go on the low setting for the day. "This is guaranteed to make your crew happy after the branding," says Terry. She ought to know. They run a big herd in Colorado, and there is a lot of branding to be done.

5 strips bacon
2 pounds ground beef
1 onion, peeled and chopped
4 ripe tomatoes, peeled and chopped
2 cloves garlic, peeled and chopped
2 tablespoons chili powder
1 (16-ounce) can tomato sauce
3 (1-pound) cans red kidney beans
Salt and pepper to taste

1. In a skillet, fry the bacon until it is crisp. Drain on a paper towel. When it is cool, cut it into pieces.

2. Add the ground beef to the skillet. Stir and cook until it is well done.

3. Add the onion, tomatoes, garlic, chili powder, tomato sauce, and beans. Cover and simmer for at least 1 hour. Then add cooked bacon.

4. Add salt and pepper to your taste. If it's really cold outside, add a dash of green Tabasco sauce.

SERVES 8

BIG EASY STEW

Down South, 'way down South, there is a ranch. On that ranch there is a cowgirl who wrangles chickens, quite a lot of chickens. She grows them organically and free range and sells them, fresh that day, to the chefs in New Orleans. "I make a run every day with fresh-killed chickens," she says. "Once I asked a chef what he did with the chickens, and this is the recipe he gave me." She prefers not to use her name in case the chef (who is really pretty famous) finds out she shared. Our gain, right?

1. Combine the paprika, granulated garlic (or powder), onion powder, dried oregano, dried thyme, cayenne, and black pepper together in a small bowl; set aside.

2. To a 5- to 6-quart slow cooker, add the red kidney beans, sweet potatoes, cut-up chicken thighs, chicken broth, peppers, both cans of tomatoes, and reserved herbs and spices. Stir together, cover, and cook on low for 8 to 9 hours or on high for 5 to 6 hours.

3. When the cooking time has elapsed, add the salt to taste. This stew is good served over rice, or in a bowl with sliced French bread for dipping. It is even better on the second day, reheated.

SERVES 4-6

2 teaspoons sweet paprika
2 teaspoons granulated garlic (garlic powder will do)
1 teaspoon onion powder
1 teaspoon dried oregano
1 teaspoon dried thyme
1/2 to 3/4 teaspoon cayenne
1/2 teaspoon ground black pepper
2 (15-ounce) cans red kidney beans, rinsed and drained
2 1/2 cups peeled, cubed sweet potatoes
1 pound boneless, skinless chicken thighs, cut into bite-size pieces
2 cups reduced-sodium chicken broth
1 1/2 cups yellow or orange sweet peppers
1 (14.5-ounce) can diced tomatoes, undrained
1 (14.5-ounce) can tomatoes and chopped green chiles, undrained
1/2 to 1 teaspoon salt

ROBIN JOHNSON

CHARMAIN'S WHITE BEAN SOUP

We asked Cowgirl Charmain to reinvent a rather boring soup recipe, and she came up with a soup that is not only reinvented but anything but boring. This is out-of-this-world hearty and satisfying!

1-2 tablespoons canola or other cooking oil
1 small onion, sliced into thin strips
2 cloves garlic, minced
Salt and pepper to taste
2 teaspoons ground cumin
1-1½ cups smoked sausage, like kielbasa, cut into bite-size pieces
1 pound skinless, boneless chicken breasts, cut into small pieces
2 tablespoons flour
8-10 cups rich chicken broth
2 (15-ounce) cans white beans (1 can great northern and 1 can white kidney make for good variety)
1 cup frozen whole-kernel corn
Salsa, for serving
Sour cream, for serving

1. Heat the oil in a large Dutch oven or heavy pot. Sauté the onion over medium heat, stirring occasionally. When onion becomes transparent and is just barely browning, add the garlic. Sauté a little longer, about 3 minutes.

2. Add the salt, pepper, and cumin, then add the sausage; cook for 2 minutes.

3. Add the chicken and sauté until the chicken releases juices and begins to brown.

CHARMAIN MURRAY

4. Stir in the flour and a little broth—enough to cover the bottom of the pan. Turn up the heat to medium-high and stir well while deglazing the yummy brown pieces on the bottom; let this reduce a little.

5. Add the beans, corn, and rest of the chicken broth. Bring to a gentle boil, then turn down to low and simmer, covered, until beans and chicken are tender, about 2 hours.

6. Check liquid level after 1 hour; if it seems low, add a little more broth. Taste and correct seasoning with salt and pepper, if necessary.

7. Serve hot with a cold, thick, chunky tomato salsa and perhaps a dollop of sour cream. Garlic bread or cheese bread for dunking is the pièce de résistance!

SERVES 6-8

The Cowgirl's Guide to Slow Cookers

Are we the very last people in the entire world to know about the joys of a slow cooker? It is possible. Change is always a challenge for us. "If it ain't broke . . ." Well, you get the idea.

That said, we have had a revelation on slow cooking! We love it! The ease and convenience of it is very attractive, and the number of recipes you can Google is simply staggering. It appears that you can cook anything at all in a slow cooker if you have the right cooker for the job.

Crock-Pot was the original slow cooker, and it is the brand name for the slow cookers made by Rival Manufacturing Company. Now there are many other brands—including KitchenAid, Cuisinart, Hamilton Beach, Bella, and others—that sell "Crock-Pot-style" slow cookers. The word Crock-Pot has become a generic word for slow cookers.

All slow cookers contain the same three components: a ceramic or porcelain pot, a glass lid, and a heating element. The pot can be round or oval and comes in various sizes.

Slow cookers use moist heat to cook food over a long period of time. They generally have just two heat settings—low wattage (bringing them to temperatures in the range of 200°F) and high wattage (bringing them to temperatures in the range of 300°F). All the recipes in this book prepared in a slow cooker were cooked in a small older-style pot that had three settings: on, off, and high. We did just fine.

We spent quite a bit of time in the appliance section of a big-box store, looking at other types of slow cookers—oval, very large, colored, and equipped with a timer. Some also had a third, lower wattage and a "warming option," which we coveted. Full disclosure : We bought an oval larger one toward the end of our cooking recipes for this book for the roasts. Yes, it has the warming option. No, it is not red. But, yes, we were tempted.

Here are some tips we have learned to make the slow cooker experience the best it can be.

- Smaller slow cookers, 1 to 3½ quarts, are perfect for one or two people.
- Medium-size cookers, between 3 and 5 quarts, will easily cook up a meal for four people.
- The large slow cooker, at 6 to 7 quarts, is good for cooking a large dinner and having leftovers the next day.
- A recipe that calls for a cooking time in the oven for 15 to 30 minutes at 350°F can be converted to 1½ to 2½ hours on the high setting of a slow cooker or 4 to 6 hours on low. Again, there are charts online to help you convert one of your old recipes from the oven to a slow cooker.
- Always, and we mean *always*, spray the pot with nonstick cooking spray before adding any ingredients. Our learning curve was cooking the grits without spray first. It took a long time to get the pot clean as a whistle, but we have to say, the grits were wonderful!

CHUCK WAGON STEW

 This recipe comes from the days when the chuck wagon went out with the crew for branding and/or gathering the cattle. Those camp cooks had to be versatile and use whatever they had. The beef was fresh, of course, but they also took along some preserved pork as well as lamb (usually mutton, or "quite-a-bit-older lamb"). We have taken some liberties with the original recipe, because, while it was filling and provided quite a bit of protein, it was, well, boring. Don't tell the camp cook, okay?

1 pound beef stew meat, cut into cubes

1 pound lamb, cut into cubes

1 pound pork, cut into cubes

Flour

¼ cup bacon fat or shortening

4 russet potatoes, peeled and diced

4 white onions, peeled and diced

1 (16-ounce) package frozen peas (or use fresh ones if you have a garden, about 2 cups)

1 (15.25-ounce) can corn (or 2 cups fresh and cut off the cob)

4 tomatoes, peeled and diced

2 cups water

¼ cup soy sauce (Don't weaken on this ingredient—it works!)

Salt and pepper

2 cups Burgundy wine

1. In a Dutch oven or Crock-Pot, brown the meat (which has been lightly dusted with flour) in the bacon fat or shortening. I prefer bacon fat for the flavor.

2. Add the vegetables, water, soy sauce, and salt and pepper. Simmer, covered, over low heat for 5 hours, or until the meats are very tender.

3. Add the wine. (See? Not boring any longer!) Simmer for 1 more hour with the lid off to allow the wine to evaporate. Add more salt and pepper to taste.

SERVES 4

COWGIRL STEW

This recipe, under many different names, has been passed around for decades. It's also known as Shipwreck Stew, 7 Layer Casserole, Cowboy Casserole, and Hobo Dinner. No matter what the name, the simplicity is what keeps cowgirls coming back to it. Layers of ground meat and vegetables soften and meld together with tomatoes during a long, slow simmer in the slow cooker or the oven. No browning or stirring or fiddling required. This recipe is very flexible and can be adapted to ingredients in your pantry. Try adding other vegetables, or a sprinkling of fresh or dried herbs, to make it your own. The amounts listed here are just guidelines.

1. Put all ingredients in a greased casserole dish in the order listed. Season with salt and pepper as you put each layer in the casserole. We used salt, pepper, and garlic powder.

2. Bake for 1½ hours in a 350°F oven with the lid on.

3. Stir it up after it has cooled a little.

Note: You can also prepare this in a slow cooker. Spray the slow cooker pot with cooking spray and layer as directed in original recipe. Cook on low for 5 hours. Then stir it up after it has cooled a little.

SERVES 6

2 medium potatoes, peeled and sliced
2 small onions, sliced
½ cup celery chopped
¼ cup raw rice
1 pound raw hamburger, crumbled
1 (16.25-ounce) can red kidney beans with juice
1 (10¾-ounce) can tomato soup
Salt and pepper to taste

FISH CHOWDER

While it is true that cowgirls eat beef, they also like other dishes. We like a good, rich, hearty fish chowder now and then. Furthermore, it has bacon in it, another great favorite of ours.

4 slices bacon, chopped
1 large carrot, peeled and chopped
2 stalks celery, peeled of the strings and chopped
1 large white potato, peeled and chopped
1/2 cup water, plus 2 tablespoons
2 small white onions, chopped
2 tablespoons all-purpose flour
1 (8-ounce) can clams, drained with liquid reserved
1 cup bottled clam juice
1 pound whitefish (such as cod, sole, or catfish), cut into 1-inch chunks (You can also add a can of drained shrimp and/or crabmeat.)
1/2 cup milk
1/2 teaspoon sea salt
1/2 teaspoon freshly ground pepper
6 slices toasted French bread for serving

1. In a large saucepan, cook the bacon on medium heat until browned and crisp, turning occasionally. Drain on paper towels and set aside. Discard all but 1 tablespoon of the bacon fat.

2. While the bacon cooks, in a large microwave-safe bowl, combine the carrot, celery, potato, and 2 tablespoons water. Cover with vented plastic wrap and microwave on high for 5 minutes, or until vegetables are just tender.

Chowder Crackers

These crackers are wonderful sprinkled on top of the Fish Chowder.
   1 (1-ounce) package ranch dressing mix
   1/4 cup canola or vegetable oil
   1/2 teaspoon garlic powder, or to taste
   Salt to taste
   1 box or bag oyster crackers

   1. Preheat the oven to 250°F.
   2. In a large mixing bowl, combine first 5 ingredients and mix well. Stir in oyster crackers and mix to coat.
   3. Pour the crackers onto a large cookie sheet. Bake 15 minutes, stirring every 5 minutes or so.

3. Keep the saucepan with the bacon fat on medium. Add the onions and cook 6 to 8 minutes, or until tender, stirring occasionally. Add the vegetables and cook for 2 minutes, stirring constantly.

4. Add the flour and cook 2 minutes more, stirring constantly. Add the clam juice, reserved clam juice, and ½ cup water and whisk until smooth. Heat to boiling, stirring occasionally.

5. Add the fish chunks, cover, and cook 4 to 5 minutes, or until the fish turns opaque throughout. Don't overcook the fish! Stir in the milk, salt, and pepper. Add the drained clams (they get tough if cooked too long). Cook 1 to 2 minutes, or until hot but not boiling. Crumble the cooled bacon and add it to the top. Serve with French bread.

SERVES 6

When a cowgirl dies and goes to Heaven, she does not get a halo. Instead, she gets a big, silver belt buckle.

—Jill Charlotte Stanford

FIT FOR A QUEEN GREEN CHILE SOUP

½ cup vegetable oil
2 pounds lean pork loin, cut into ½-inch cubes
1 cup flour, mixed with salt and pepper to taste for dredging the pork
2 tablespoons minced garlic
2 cups diced onions
3 cups diced tomatoes
2 cups canned green chiles, seeded and diced
1 cup tomato juice
1 cup water
1 tablespoon Tabasco sauce
1 tablespoon ground coriander
Salt and pepper to taste

1. Heat the oil in a large skillet or Dutch oven.

2. Dredge the meat in the flour until well coated. Add to the heated oil and brown on all sides.

3. Add the garlic and onion to the meat and simmer until the onions are tender. Stir often, getting all the bits from the bottom of the pan.

4. Add the tomatoes, chiles, tomato juice, water, Tabasco sauce, and coriander. Simmer until the meat is tender, about 1 hour. Add salt and pepper if necessary.

SERVES 6-8

Our perfect companions have never fewer than four feet.

—Colette

HEARTY VEGETABLE SOUP

Robin Johnson is my sister, and she asked how she could help with the book, Keep Cookin' Cowgirl. I asked for a really good vegetable soup, and here it is again, back by popular demand. She says, "Through the years I have fooled around with this recipe, and it comes out differently each time, because it all depends on what is in the fridge and what I have on hand. Have fun with it. It's quick, easy, and really good on the second day."

1. Heat the olive oil in a large soup pot. Add the onion, carrots, and celery. Cook on medium-low heat for about 10 minutes, until the onion is translucent.

2. Add the zucchini and oregano or basil and continue to sauté for a few minutes. Add the stock and bring to a boil, then reduce to a simmer for another 10 minutes, or until the zucchini is cooked.

3. Add the cabbage and cook for a few minutes, then add the tomatoes and both beans. Bring the soup back up to temperature—but don't let it boil. Add the remaining seasonings carefully, tasting until you like what you've got! Serve with grated Parmesan or other cheese if desired.

SERVES 8 WITH PLENTY LEFT OVER

ROBIN JOHNSON

2 tablespoons olive oil
1 cup diced yellow onion
1 cup diced carrots
1 cup diced celery
1 cup diced zucchini
1½ teaspoons oregano and/
   or basil
1 (14.5-ounce) can vegetable
   or chicken stock
1 cup shredded cabbage (cut
   into ½-inch strips)
1 (14.5-ounce) can diced
   tomatoes with juice
1 (14.5-ounce) can kidney
   beans, drained and rinsed
1 (14.5-ounce) can green
   beans, drained
5–7 drops hot sauce, or to
   taste
1 teaspoon salt
⅛ teaspoon pepper
Parmesan or other cheese for
   serving (optional)

SHEEPHERDERS' LAMB SHANK STEW

My very first cookbook was *Lamb Country Cooking*. I am a big fan of lamb. I know that there were terrible conflicts between the sheepherders and the cattlemen in the early days, but no matter what you were trailing, you still had to stop and eat. Try this soup/stew dish with some crusty bread.

6 cups water or organic chicken broth
1 cup dry split peas, green or yellow
4 lamb shanks (no need to braise or brown first)
1 teaspoon thyme or rosemary
1 large garlic clove, sliced
1 teaspoon salt
6 crushed peppercorns
1 tablespoon rice, brown or white
2 large carrots, peeled and cut into rounds
1 large onion, coarsely chopped

1. Mix all the ingredients in a slow cooker (be sure to coat the inside with nonstick cooking spray first) or a heavy ovenproof casserole with a lid.

2. If using a casserole dish, bake in a preheated 300°F oven for 3 hours, or until the meat is tender. Cook on high for 3 to 4 hours if using a slow cooker. Add more water if it gets too thick.

3. The shanks are perfect when they are tender. Prick them with a fork, and if they are nearly falling off the bone, they're ready!

SERVES 4

HIGH DESERT POTATO AND BACON SOUP

Many women out on the plains and deserts had to "make do" with what was at hand and come up with satisfying meals. All the ingredients in this soup are "to hand" (as they used to say), and it is very satisfying! This recipe comes from a shepherd's daughter who spent the first six years of her life in a covered wagon following a vast herd of sheep over the hills of the High Desert of Central Oregon.

1. Cook the potatoes and onion in water until soft. Then "mash" them a little bit to release more flavor, but do not drain. Add salt and pepper to taste.

2. Cut the bacon into small pieces and fry until crisp and brown. Remove the bacon from the fat to drain. Add the bread crumbs to the fat and stir and toast until brown.

3. Add the cooked bacon and browned bread crumbs to the potato and onion soup and reheat, adding more seasonings if you wish. Stir in the cream or evaporated milk.

SERVES 6

3 large potatoes, peeled and cubed
1 medium onion, peeled and cubed
1 quart water
Salt and pepper to taste
5 strips bacon
1½ cups bread crumbs from stale bread
½ cup cream (evaporated milk will do)

PUMPKIN SOUP

In less than 15 minutes, from start to finish, you can enjoy this tasty pumpkin soup, which calls for just five ingredients. Everyone will look for the remains of the pumpkin you hollowed out, baked, and pureed. We won't tell if you won't.

4 cups of pumpkin puree—
   not pumpkin pie mix
2 cups chicken stock
1 cup half and half
1 tablespoon ground ginger
2 teaspoons cinnamon
Salt and pepper to taste
2 tablespoons curry powder,
   instead of the ginger and
   cinnamon (optional)
Sour cream for serving
   (optional)
Pumpkin seeds for serving
   (optional)

1. Whisk all of the ingredients together in a medium saucepan. Make sure there are no clumps. Heat over medium heat for about 15 minutes. Allow this to simmer a little longer for the flavors to get it all together. You can also put all of the ingredients in a slow cooker and cook on low for 1 hour.

2. Dress up the soup when you serve it in a cup or a bowl by adding a dollop of sour cream and/or roasted pumpkin seeds. Sprinkle parsley for garnish.

SERVES 2

JILL STANFORD

JUNIPER CHILI

 Nicole Carter lives in Homedale, Idaho. She has two darling children and a job "with the Feds," she says. But this cowgirl is also an avid hunter. She says, "I shot my first whitetail, a 4x5 buck, with a Remington 270. I like to hunt turkey and pheasants, too. I made this chili for a chili cook-off and came in second!"

You can make this with elk or deer burger meat or beef stew meat. We are in awe of her hunting skills as well as her cooking prowess!

Mix all the ingredients in a slow cooker and cook on low for 6 hours.

SERVES 6

You don't win buckles for a clean house.

—Anonymous

1½ cups great northern beans, dried and washed

1½ cups white butter beans, dried and washed

1½ cups white kidney beans, dried and washed

1½ cups white shoepeg (white kernel) corn

1½ cups black-eyed peas

2 cups beef broth

1 medium sweet onion, chopped

1 stalk celery, chopped

1–2 tablespoons roasted garlic

1 pound elk or deer burger meat or stew meat

2–3 cups torn or chopped fresh cilantro

1–2 tablespoons cumin

Salt and fresh ground pepper

Secret ingredient: 1 tablespoon or to taste juniper berry and peppercorn rub that you order from www.wildeats.com. Just pour directly into the slow cooker. (It's a blend of African black peppercorns, juniper berries, salt, and garlic.)

CASSEROLES AND HOT DISHES

AFTER-EASTER CASSEROLE

One of our favorite sayings is, "The definition of Eternity is one ham and two people." This ought to help.

1½ pounds cooked ham, sliced about ¼-inch thick

3 pounds cooked yams or sweet potatoes, sliced

1 (8-ounce) can sliced pineapple, drained and cut in half

½ cup chopped pecans

¾ cup maple syrup

1. Preheat the oven to 350°F. Arrange ham slices, yam or potato slices, and pineapple slices alternately in a buttered casserole dish. Sprinkle the pecans on top.

2. Bake uncovered for 15 minutes. Remove from oven and pour the syrup over the casserole. Return to the oven and bake for 20 minutes more.

SERVES 6

If I had it all to do over again, what would I do different? Be just a little bit wilder—ride more wild horses.

—Martha Stranahan

COWGIRL'S CHICKEN POT PIE

We wound up with quite a few cans of canned green peas. They were cheap! The pea soup we devised was terrific, but then what? Chicken potpie, and we really do mean "pie"! Once again, prepackaged baking mix has proven to us that it should be a staple in every cowgirl's pantry, especially if she has quite a few cans of peas.

1. Preheat the oven to 400°F. In an ungreased 9-inch pie plate, stir together the peas, mixed vegetables, chicken, and soup.

2. In a medium bowl, stir the baking mix, milk, egg, garlic salt, and salt and pepper until blended. Pour on top of the veggies in the pie plate.

3. Bake uncovered for about 30 minutes, or until the crust is golden brown. Let the pie rest before cutting, about 5 minutes.

SERVES 6

1 (15-ounce) can green peas, drained
1 (15-ounce) can mixed vegetables, drained
1 cup cooked and diced chicken
1 (10¾-ounce) can cream of chicken soup
1 cup baking mix
½ cup milk
1 egg
1 tablespoon garlic salt
Salt and pepper to taste

JILL S"ANFORD

Mabel Strickland: The First Lady of Rodeo

Mabel DeLong Strickland, born in 1897, started her career as a trick rider at the Walla Walla Frontier Days in Washington State in 1913. It has been said that Mabel was the most beloved cowgirl in early day rodeo. She was beautiful and had a poise not often seen while on top of a bucking saddle bronc. She also competed in steer roping and relay racing, against both cowboys and cowgirls, and set several world records. Mabel went to Hollywood and performed in the movies, doing stunt work for leading actors and actresses. She won more world titles than any other cowgirl in the business. She was the winner of the prestigious McAlpin Trophy in 1922 (Cheyenne's All-Around Cowgirl), and she was a fan favorite at the First Madison Square Garden Rodeo in 1922. She was the Queen of the Pendleton Round-Up in 1927.

DIVINE TURKEY

When Jill's son, Charlie, was a little cowboy, he would not eat broccoli except in this casserole. We know a few grownup cowboys and cowgirls who won't eat broccoli either—except in this dish. Charlie called it Divine Turkey, and it was always served a few days after Thanksgiving, freeing up the turkey carcass for the soup I made the next day. It's fast and, yes, it uses cream of chicken soup, but when you have livestock to feed, not to mention a hungry family, this is a life-saver with no leftovers. (You can use leftover chicken, too, and I have even run into it at a pot-luck with leftover ham as the meat. Cream of celery soup also makes it quite good!)

1. Preheat the oven to 450°F. In a 2-quart baking dish, spread out the broccoli and leftover turkey.

2. In a small bowl, mix the soup, milk, and pepper. Pour this over the broccoli and turkey, then sprinkle the cheese evenly over all.

3. Bake for 15 minutes or until the cheese is melted and bubbly.

SERVES 4

4 cups cooked broccoli florets, drained
2 cups leftover turkey, cut into cubes
1 (10¾-ounce) can cream of chicken soup
½ cup milk
¼ teaspoon pepper
½ cup shredded cheddar cheese

COWGIRL GARDEN SUMMER PIE

For the pie crust

1½ cups prepared baking mix

¼ cup soft butter

3 tablespoons boiling water

For the pie filling

3 tomatoes (about 2 pounds), sliced in ½-inch slices

1 medium Walla Walla or Vidalia sweet onion

1 cup yellow or white corn, fresh or frozen

½ cup mayonnaise

2 tablespoons fresh lemon juice (you can cheat)

1 tablespoon parsley (fresh if you have it, but dried is fine)

1 tablespoon basil (fresh if you have it, but dried is fine)

1½ cups sharp cheddar cheese, grated, divided

Salt and pepper to taste

½ cup crisp bacon bits

2 tablespoons chopped green onions

1. Preheat the oven to 375°F. To prepare the pie crust put the baking mix and butter in a medium bowl and mix with a fork until it is a crumble. Add the boiling water and stir with the fork and then your hands until you can form the dough into a ball (add a little more water if it isn't soft enough).

2. Press the pie dough into a 9-inch glass or ceramic pie plate until it is evenly distributed on the bottom and up the sides of the dish. Flute the edges. Then place the pie crust in the freezer for 15 minutes. Take it out and bake for 8 to 10 minutes. Let it cool and set aside while you get "the innards" ready.

3. To prepare the pie filling, cut the tomatoes into ½-inch-thick slices and spread on a baking pan lined with paper towels. Sprinkle a small amount of salt over the tomatoes and then cover with paper towels. Let tomatoes drain on the counter for 30 minutes or longer.

4. Rough chop the onion and then sauté with a small amount of butter until it just starts to brown. Set aside.

5. In a small bowl, mix the mayonnaise with the lemon juice, 1 cup of the cheese, and the parsley and basil. Add salt and pepper to taste.

6. Brush the bottom of the pie crust with a small amount of the mayonnaise spread. Then arrange the sliced tomatoes in a layer on the bottom of the crust. Sprinkle the onions and corn on the tomatoes and then carefully spread the rest of the mayonnaise mix on top. Arrange the rest of the tomatoes on top of the spread. Sprinkle with the bacon, the remaining cheese, and the green onions.

7. Bake the pie on the center rack of the oven for 40 to 45 minutes. At 30 minutes, if the crust is browning up, cover lightly with tin foil and continue baking until hot and bubbly. Let the pie cool for 15 minutes. Enjoy hot or at room temperature.

MAKES 1 8" OR 9" PIE

Variation: Add 1 cup of cooked leftover chicken after the corn and onions and continue with the recipe, topping this with the tomatoes, cheese, bacon, and green onions.

ROEIN JOHNSON

JOAN'S CHILES RELLENOS

Joan Triplett has been described as the "iron butterfly." No bigger than a minute, she has more energy per square ounce than most cowboys. Without a hair out of place, perfectly manicured nails, and an enthusiastic, adventuresome spirit, she is the quintessential cowgirl in our eyes. To sit in front of a real log fire by her massive river-rock fireplace is to enjoy what is the truest spirit of the West.

3 (7-ounce) cans whole green chiles
1 pound Monterey Jack cheese, grated
1 pound cheddar cheese, grated
3 eggs
3 tablespoons flour
1 (12-ounce) can evaporated milk
1 (15-ounce) can tomato sauce
Salsa for serving
Sour cream for serving

1. Wash the chiles, remove any seeds, and pat dry.

2. In a 9x13-inch baking pan, layer half of the chiles and half of the cheeses. Repeat layers, reserving ½ cup of cheese for topping.

3. In a medium bowl, beat the eggs. Add the flour and milk and beat until blended.

4. Pour the egg mixture over the chiles and cheese. The casserole can be refrigerated at this point while you go for a ride.

5. Bake the casserole at 350°F for 30 minutes. Remove from the oven, spread the tomato sauce evenly over the top, sprinkle with the reserved cheese, and then bake for 15 minutes longer. Let the casserole cool for 10 minutes, then cut into squares to serve with salsa and sour cream, if desired.

SERVES 6

JILL STANFORD

RIMROCK TOMATO MAC AND CHEESE

As kids, we loved mac and cheese. As grownups (sorta), we love this!

1. Cook macaroni according to package directions and drain. Set aside. Preheat oven to 350°F.

2. To make the sauce, melt the butter in a saucepan. Blend in the flour. Cook and stir on medium heat for about 2 minutes, then add the milk and stir constantly until it thickens.

3. Stir in the cheddar cheese and then the cooked macaroni. Add salt and pepper to taste. Mix well.

4. Pour the macaroni and cheese into a baking dish coated with nonstick cooking spray. Arrange sliced tomatoes on top and then sprinkle with Parmesan cheese.

5. Bake uncovered 20 to 25 minutes, or until bubbling and starting to brown.

SERVES 4

2 cups uncooked macaroni
3 tablespoons butter
3 tablespoons flour
2 cups milk
2 cups shredded cheddar cheese
1/4 teaspoon salt
Fresh ground pepper to taste
2 ripe tomatoes, sliced
1/4 cup grated Parmesan cheese

ZUCCHINI AND HAM PIE

Too many zucchini in your garden? This ought to take care of the problem. In fact, this will be requested again. Good for breakfast, lunch, or dinner. (Just wait until you see how the crust is made!)

For the pie crust
1½ cups all-purpose flour
1½ teaspoons sugar
   (optional)
½ teaspoon salt
½ cup canola oil
3 tablespoons ice water

For the filling
2 tablespoons olive oil
2 medium zucchini, halved
   lengthwise, then cut into
   ⅛-inch thick slices
½ cup diced sweet onion
½ cup sweet red pepper, cut
   into 1- or 2-inch slices, ⅛-
   inch thick
3 large eggs
½ cup whole milk
¾ cup heavy cream
¼ pound cooked ham, cut
   into ½-inch pieces
2 cups shredded Swiss
   cheese
Salt and pepper to taste

1. Preheat the oven to 375°F. To make the pie crust, mix the dry ingredients together in a medium bowl. Make a well in the center and add the oil and ice water. Stir with a fork until well combined.

2. Spread the pie dough evenly over a 9-inch pie plate (preferably glass) and pat it with your fingers until it covers both the bottom and the sides of the pie plate, creating a decorative or plain edge at the top. Prick the bottom of the crust with a fork a number of times and then place a round circle of parchment paper, the same size as the pie plate, in the crust and fill with dry beans or rice. Put the crust in the refrigerator for 30 minutes.

3. Place the chilled pie crust on the center rack of the oven and bake for 15 minutes. Take it out of the oven and put it on a rack to cool. When it's cooled a bit, you can take the parchment paper and weights out of the crust, and it's ready to be filled.

4. Turn up the oven to 450°F. In a large skillet, heat the oil and sauté the zucchini, onion, and red pepper on medium-high heat until cooked (about 5 to 7 minutes), stirring frequently.

5. Whisk the eggs in a large bowl until frothy.

6. Heat the milk and cream in a small pan until hot, but not boiling. Add a small amount of the hot liquid to the eggs and then slowly add the rest.

7. Add the cooked vegetables, ham, and Swiss cheese to the bowl. Add salt and pepper as you like and then place the mixture into your prepared pie crust, being careful to not overfill the crust.

8. Bake on the center rack for 25 to 30 minutes, or until the egg is set.

Cool on a wire rack.

MAKES ONE PIE

ROBIN JOHNSON

TAD'S SPECIAL

Barbara Inez (Tad) Lucas of Fort Worth, Texas, the youngest of twenty-four children, was considered one of the greatest professional cowgirls of all time. She won all of the major trophies and titles available to rodeo cowgirls from 1917 through the late 1920s. She was a fearless and innovative trick rider and toured in Wild West shows throughout the United States and Europe. She died in 1990, one of the last of the great cowgirls.

This dish is awfully good with flour tortillas or in taco shells. It is quick and easy and just the thing after a good ride on a mean bronc.

1 pound ground beef
1 medium onion, chopped
1 cup cooked spinach, drained
    well and chopped fine
Salt to taste
2 eggs, beaten
Pepper to taste
6 tortillas or taco shells
1 cup grated Monterey Jack
    cheese
Toppings of your choice,
    including sour cream,
    guacamole, chopped black
    olives, and/or chopped
    chiles or peppers.

1. In a large skillet, brown the beef and onion. Stir in the spinach and salt. Simmer for 10 minutes.

2. Add the beaten eggs and stir with a fork until the eggs are set. Add pepper.

3. Place a large spoonful of the mixture on a warm tortilla or in a taco shell. Top with a sprinkle of cheese. You can go on and on with this by topping it off with sour cream, guacamole, chopped black olives, and/or chopped chiles or peppers.

SERVES 6

CHARMAIN MURRAY

COWGIRLS IN THE KITCHEN

THE BUNKHOUSE FAVORITE TUNA-EGG CASSEROLE

Cowgirl Charmain Murray kitchen-tested this for us. She made some suggestions, all of which we thought were just right for this easy-to-do and comforting casserole. Looks good, doesn't it?

1. Preheat oven to 350°F. Cook the noodles according to package directions. Drain.

2. Melt the butter in a small skillet. Sauté the celery in the butter until almost tender.

3. In a medium bowl, combine the soup and ½ cup of water. Add the tuna and lemon peel, if using. Then add a handful (about ½ cup) of the cheese and mix well. Next add three of the sliced eggs, saving one for the top. Finally, add the noodles and combine well.

4. Spoon the mixture into a 1-quart casserole dish and bake for 30 minutes. Garnish the top with the remaining cheese and egg slices.

SERVES 4

1 cup uncooked Fusilli "curly" noodles
2 tablespoons butter
1 cup chopped celery
1 can cream of mushroom or cream of celery soup
1 can tuna, drained
2 teaspoons grated lemon peel (but only if you have it)
1 cup shredded cheese, divided
4 hard-boiled eggs, sliced, divided

CHARMAIN MURRAY

CHICKEN AND FISH

METOLIUS RIVER SALMON LOAF

One of the great mysteries of a cowgirl's pantry is why there is always—and we mean always—a can of tinned salmon in it. If you scrounge around enough, you might also find a box of saltine crackers. Add a few other things found in every cowgirl's pantry, and you are on your way to a delicious casserole, like the one we were served as luncheon fare by a woman who was retired from the rigors of ranch life and told hair-raising tales of pulling calves in snowstorms and loose cinches. The background music to this pleasant afternoon was the sound of the Metolius River rushing by her cabin.

1 egg
¼ cup undiluted evaporated milk
1 cup crumbled saltine crackers or soft bread crumbs
1 tablespoon butter, melted
Salt and pepper to taste
2 cups tinned salmon, drained and flaked
Tomato sauce or mayonnaise for serving

1. Preheat the oven to 400°F. Beat together the egg, milk, crumbled crackers or bread crumbs, melted butter, salt, and pepper.

2. Add the salmon to the crumb mixture and stir together. Pour mixture into a greased loaf pan. Bake for 30 minutes or until set. Serve hot with tomato sauce, or sliced cold with mayonnaise.

SERVES 6

JILL STANFORD

FRIDAY NIGHT FISH

This is going to be your secret recipe. You will not tell a soul, ever, how you made this moist and delicious fish. No one will ever guess how you did this, except for Marjorie Rogers. Unless, of course, they buy this book and read the directions . . .

1. Preheat the oven to 375°F. Coat a 9 x 11-inch glass baking dish with oil or cooking spray.

2. Lay the fish flat in the baking dish. Using a spatula, spread a layer of mayonnaise on the fish like you would on a sandwich, as thick or as thin as you like. (Us? Pretty thick!)

JILL STANFORD

1 tablespoon vegetable oil, or any cooking spray
4 (8- to 10-ounce) pieces fresh or frozen whitefish, such as haddock or cod
½ cup mayonnaise (the real stuff)
½ cup bread crumbs, plain or seasoned
1 lemon, thinly sliced
1 cup white wine or water
Salt and freshly ground pepper to taste
Parsley (optional)

3. Sprinkle the coated fish with the bread crumbs, then lay the lemon slices on top. Pour the white wine or water all around the fish to add moisture, covering the bottom of the pan.

4. Bake the fish, uncovered, for about 15 to 20 minutes, or until the fish is done. It's done when it's white in the middle, not opaque, and flakes easily.

5. Sprinkle salt, freshly ground pepper, and chopped fresh parsley to taste.

SERVES 4

KRABBY KAKES

Growing up in Washington State, near Puget Sound, we have a deep affection for all things seafood. But now we live far away from salt water. Still, we can re-create a taste of those salty times with this easy and quick recipe. Serve with tartar sauce, which you can easily make by adding relish (the green kind) to mayonnaise, to taste. A wedge of lemon is nice too, for its "bite."

2 slices dried bread (crusts and all)
3 tablespoons milk
1 tablespoon mayonnaise
1 tablespoon Worcestershire sauce
1 tablespoon baking powder
1 tablespoon parsley flakes
1 teaspoon Old Bay® Seasoning
1/4 teaspoon salt
1/4 teaspoon lemon pepper
1 tablespoon minced, dried onion
1 egg beaten
1 (16-ounce) can crabmeat
Oil for frying, such as canola

1. Break the bread into very small pieces in a large bowl. Moisten with the milk.

Add the mayonnaise and Worcestershire sauce; mix well. Add remaining ingredients; mix lightly.

2. Shape mixture into 4 patties.

3. Refrigerate the patties 30 minutes to help keep them together when cooking.

4. Fry in 2 inches of hot oil until golden brown on both sides. Ahoy!

MAKES 4 PATTIES

JILL STANFORD

SEASIDE SLOW COOKER FISH

 Can you cook fish in a slow cooker? You certainly can, using this recipe. One of our "official tasters" was amazed at how good this was. You will be too.

1. Cut the fish into 2 or 3 small pieces (about the size of a deck of cards). Cut off a piece of aluminum foil large enough to completely wrap around the fish and lay it on the counter.

2. Put the carrots and celery on the foil and then lay the fish on the vegetables. Salt and pepper the fish and then lay the pats of butter and the lemon rounds on top of it all.

3. Fold up the foil so that the fish is still lying flat and you can crimp the foil together to seal it up tightly. (Just before you crimp the packets, add the wine if you want.)

4. Place the foil packet into a 5- to 6-quart slow cooker and cook on low for 3 hours, or until the fish flakes and is opaque.

SERVES 2-3

1 pound cod or halibut
1 stalk celery, cut into thin sticks
1 small carrot, cut into thin sticks
1/2 lemon, cut into rounds
Salt and pepper to taste
2 pats butter
1/4 cup white wine (optional)

ROBIN JOHNSON

TUNA FISH PATTIES

We are daughters of a tugboat captain. We all love seafood. We like these tuna patties mother made and that Robin improved. You will too. We ate them on a bun with mayonnaise and lettuce, while Robin served them as simply a patty with tomato and cucumber—a little salad. You could whip up a simple tartar sauce by combining mayonnaise and hamburger relish to taste too.

3 (5-ounce) cans water-packed tuna (drained)
2 teaspoons Dijon mustard
1/2 cup bread crumbs
1 teaspoon lemon zest
1 tablespoon lemon juice
2 tablespoons chopped parsley
2 tablespoons chopped green onions
1/2 teaspoon Tabasco sauce (hot sauce)
1/3 cup mayonnaise
Salt and pepper to taste
2 tablespoons olive oil
1 teaspoon butter

1. In a medium bowl, combine all the ingredients (through the salt and pepper) and mix together lightly, but well.

2. Divide the mixture to make four parts. Form each part into a ball and then flatten into a patty. Put the patties on a plate with wax paper or parchment paper and let them chill for 30 minutes to an hour. Chilling helps them stay together when cooking.

JILL STANFORD

3. Heat the olive oil and butter (for taste) in a cast-iron or nonstick skillet on medium-high. When the skillet is hot, gently place the patties in the pan and cook until they are nicely browned, about 3 to 4 minutes on each side.

MAKES 4 PATTIES

Mattie Goff Newcombe—Riding at Speed

The heroine and idol of young cowgirls of her era, Mattie was a rodeo champion admired by all. Mattie participated in bronc riding, trick riding, and relay racing during her rodeo career. The first rodeo Mattie participated in was at Sioux Falls, South Dakota, in 1921. Her trick-riding skills were self-taught. She perfected her tricks, and the speed at which she performed them took your breath away. Mattie was soon nicknamed "the fastest trick rider on the fastest horse around."

During her career Mattie had three main horses: Bob, Pal, and Buster. She performed such tricks as the Roman Stand, Under the Neck, Under the Belly, Slick Saddle Stand, Back Drag, Spin the Horn, and many others. The most dangerous was the Back Drag. This stunt required Mattie to place a foot in a loop on either side of the saddle, bend backward over the rear of the horse until her hands touched the ground, and then pulling herself into an upright position unassisted.

Mattie retired from her rodeo career in the late 1930s, but not before earning the title of All-Around Cowgirl and World Champion Trick Rider several times. She was inducted into the National Cowboy Hall of Fame and the South Dakota Hall of Fame, and the Casey Tibbs Foundation honored her at their Tribute Dinner in 1991. Mattie was inducted into the National Cowgirl Hall of Fame and Western Heritage Center in Fort Worth, Texas in November 1994, as well as the National Cowgirl Hall of Fame.

Mattie Goff Newcombe DENVER PUBLIC LIBRARY

SLOW COOKER BEER-AND-BARBECUE PULLED CHICKEN SLIDERS

 Robin really knocked it out of the arena with this recipe for pulled chicken sliders! Using the barbeque sauce from The Cowgirls Cookbook, as well as the coleslaw (which you will have to make ahead of time and keep in the 'fridge), these sliders will have people lined up for more. Wahoo!

1 tablespoon sweet or smoked paprika

2 teaspoons chili powder

½ teaspoon cinnamon

2½ pounds boneless, skinless chicken breasts

12 ounces wheat beer (such as hefeweizen)

2 tablespoons honey

2 cups barbeque sauce (such as Keepin' It Simple Barbeque Sauce on page 168)

Cowgirl Coleslaw (found on page 72)

6–8 buns

1. Mix the paprika, chili powder, and cinnamon together and rub the chicken with the mixture. Then place the rubbed chicken in a 5-quart slow cooker.

2. Gently mix the beer, honey, and barbeque sauce together and pour this over the chicken in the slow cooker.

3. Cover and cook on low for 6 to 7 hours or on high for 4 to 5 hours. If the sauce gets too thick, add a little more beer.

4. When the chicken is done, lift it out of the sauce and, using two forks, shred (pull) the chicken and place it on a platter and set aside.

5. Pour the remaining sauce in a shallow skillet, bring to a boil, and reduce the sauce until it thickens slightly (to about the consistency of regular barbeque sauce you buy in a bottle). Set aside.

6. Serve the pulled chicken on slider buns (dinner rolls work) or regular larger buns. Pour some of the reduced barbeque sauce on top and then finish it with a good dollop of Cowgirl Coleslaw.

SERVES 6–8

SLOW COOKER TURKEY BREAST

 If you have not discovered a turkey breast instead of an entire turkey, then remember this recipe the next time you want turkey. No legs or wings to deal with—a bit of dark meat on the sides—we will never do a whole turkey again. Robin cooked this in her slow cooker and said, "Wow! So good and moist and I have a lot of turkey left over!"

½ cup rough-chopped onion
½ cup rough-chopped celery
¼ cup rough-chopped carrot
1 teaspoon ground sage
1 teaspoon ground marjoram
½ teaspoon ground thyme
1 teaspoon kosher salt
½ teaspoon ground black
    pepper
½ to 1 teaspoon paprika
5-6 pounds, bone-in, skin-on
    turkey breast
Olive oil

1. Spray a 6-quart oblong slow cooker with nonstick cooking spray. Put the rough-cut vegetables in the bottom.

2. Combine the sage, marjoram, thyme, salt, pepper, and paprika in a small bowl.

3. Unwrap the turkey and pat dry. Rub completely with olive oil and then rub the herb mixture on the breast. Place the breast, skin side up, on top of the vegetables (arranged so that the lid fits on snugly).

4. Turn the cooker on high and cook for 1 hour, then turn the cooker down to low and cook another 5 to 6 hours, or until the breast meat, at its thickest part, measures 165°F on an insta-read thermometer. When the turkey is done, let it cool slightly and remove the breast to a cookie sheet to brown and crisp the skin under the broiler (watch this—it happens quickly). Strain the juices to make gravy or simply serve the juices with the turkey.

SERVES 4-6

BEEF, LAMB, AND PORK

IT'S WHAT'S FOR DINNER
BEEF SHORT RIBS

 This is a recipe you will thank your slow cooker for every time you make it, and we can assure you, the hands on the ranch will ask for it again and again. No slow cooker? A heavy Dutch oven or casserole dish with a lid, in the oven at 275°F, will do just fine.

1/2 cup all-purpose flour
Salt and pepper
2 1/2 pounds beef short ribs
1/4 cup butter
1 cup chopped onion
1 cup beef broth
3/4 cup water
3/4 cup brown sugar
2 tablespoons catsup
2 tablespoons
    Worcestershire sauce
2 tablespoons minced garlic
1 teaspoon chili powder

1. Put the flour, salt, and pepper in a paper bag. Add the ribs and shake to coat.

2. Brown the ribs in the butter in a large skillet, then put them in a slow cooker or Dutch oven that has been sprayed with nonstick cooking spray.

3. In the same skillet used to brown the ribs, sauté the onion until it is nearly transparent, then add remaining ingredients. Stir until the mixture comes to nearly a boil.

4. Pour the mixture over the ribs. Cover and cook on low for 8 hours, or until the meat is falling off the bones.

SERVES 4

CHIPPED BEEF ON TOAST

You know the "other" name for this easy dish, especially if you served in the armed forces. No matter what it's called, we still think this is a great comfort dish, to be served after a hard day.

1. Melt the butter in a large pan over medium-high heat.

2. Tear the chipped beef into small pieces and add it to the butter. Cook on medium heat for 10 to 12 minutes, or until the edges begin to curl.

3. Gradually add the flour to the pan, stirring until a thick paste forms.

4. Pour in the half and half and reduce heat to medium-low. Continue stirring until the gravy becomes thick and creamy. Cook for at least 20 minutes, stirring occasionally.

5. Toast 4 to 6 pieces of bread. Spoon the chipped beef over the toast.

SERVES 4-6

⅓ cup butter
1 (5-ounce) jar dried chipped beef
3 tablespoons all-purpose flour
3½ cups half and half (or milk or cream)
Pepper to taste

My task in life is to be a happy woman.

—Sally Conners, Montana horsewoman

EASIEST POT ROAST EVER

The snow is starting to fall outside, it's colder than heck, and you have to be outside all day checking fences. You really want to come home to something hot and stick-to-your-ribs good. This is it. Like having Cookie in your cabin waiting for you to stumble in the door with a frozen nose.

This recipe uses chuck roast, but it works really well with elk too!

4- or 5-pound chuck roast
1 (1-ounce) packet ranch
   dressing mix
1 (.6-ounce) packet au jus mix
1 stick butter

1. Coat a slow cooker with nonstick cooking spray. Put the chuck roast in the slow cooker.

2. Sprinkle the ranch dressing mix on top of the roast. Then sprinkle the au jus mix on top of that.

3. Put the butter on top. Then cover the slow cooker and cook the roast on low for about 8 hours.

4. Go outside.

5. Come back in 8 hours, take off your boots, and wash your hands.

6. Remove the roast to a platter.

7. Serve the roast sliced into thick slices over a piece of bread in the bottom of a bowl. Ladle the juice over it all.

8. Have a second helping.

SERVES 4-6

JILL STANFORD

EMERGENCY STEAK

The snow is three feet deep, your nose is running, and you are starving for something fast, good, and packed with protein. Try this. You might be surprised at how good this "faux steak" is.

1. Smush all the ingredients—except the mushrooms and barbeque sauce—together with your (washed) wet hands and place on a lightly greased cast-iron frying pan. Pat the mixture into the shape of a 1-inch-thick T-bone steak.

2. Broil until rare, medium rare, or well done on one side. Carefully take the pan out and turn the meat over. This would be the time to spread some of the barbecue sauce on top if you like.

3. Continue to broil until nearly done. Put the mushrooms on top and broil for 2 minutes longer.

SERVES 4 (AND GREAT AS LEFTOVERS CRUMBLED INTO A QUICK GRAVY MIX)

1 pound hamburger
2 tablespoons minced onion
½ cup milk
Salt and pepper to taste
Dash of Worcestershire sauce, or more if you like it
¼ cup bread crumbs
1 (6.5-ounce) can mushroom stems and pieces
Keepin' It Simple Barbecue Sauce (page 168) (optional)

JILL STANFORD

MEAT LOAF IN THE SLOW LANE

Well, if this isn't just the best news! You can make a meat loaf in your "new best friend," the slow cooker. This was shared with us by Liz Sherman, a cowgirl who loves old-fashioned food but hasn't the time to wait around for the bell to ring on the oven timer. "Besides," she points out, "in the summer, who wants a hot oven going?" Good point! We tried this and liked it. We think you will too. Easily lifted out of the cooker and placed on a platter with the vegetables all around, this goes from cooker to table nicely!

3 large carrots, scraped of their skin and cut into rough pieces

2 russet potatoes, peeled and cut into rough pieces

2 pounds lean ground beef

1/2 pound pork sausage

1 large onion, finely chopped

1 1/2 cups ketchup, divided

3/4 cup seasoned bread crumbs

2 eggs

1 teaspoon garlic powder, divided

2 tablespoons Worcestershire sauce

2 teaspoons salt

1 teaspoon pepper

1/4 cup light brown sugar

1/2 teaspoon yellow mustard

1. Place the carrots and potatoes in the bottom of a 3- to 5-quart slow cooker.

2. Combine the beef, sausage, onions, 3/4 cup ketchup, bread crumbs, eggs, 1/2 teaspoon garlic powder, Worcestershire sauce, and salt and pepper in a large bowl. Use your hands to mix and make sure everything is well mixed.

3. Form the meat mixture into a loaf that is the same size as the interior of the slow cooker and gently place it over the vegetables.

4. In the same bowl, mix together the sugar, mustard, the remaining ketchup, and 1/2 teaspoon garlic powder. Spread this mixture over the top of the loaf, cover, and cook on low for 8 hours (or overnight) or on high for 4 hours.

5. Let the meat loaf sit for 15 minutes after turning off the heat, then serve warm.

SERVES 6

JILL STANFORD

LEG OF LAMB DONE SLOWLY

 When you braise lamb in the slow cooker, it becomes very tender and soooo delicious! This is a one-dish party dish for sure! We think it will change minds about not liking lamb.

1. Spray the inside of a 5-, 6-, or 7-quart slow cooker with nonstick spray.

2. In a medium bowl, combine the broth, flour, tomato paste, basil, oregano, garlic powder, pepper, and salt. Pour this mixture into the slow cooker.

3. Add the potatoes and carrots, spreading them out in one layer.

4. Heat the olive oil in a large skillet. Brown the leg of lamb well on all sides. This takes about 8 to 10 minutes. Then place the lamb on top of the vegetables.

5. Cook the onion in the same large skillet, stirring until the onion is quite soft. Add the vinegar-water mixture and stir. Cook for 2 minutes.

6. Pour the onion mixture over the lamb and vegetables, cover, and cook on high for 3 to 4 hours or low for 7 to 8 hours.

7. Move the lamb to a platter, arrange the wonderfully cooked vegetables around it, and then ladle the broth over all.

SERVES 8

1 cup beef or vegetable broth
1/4 cup flour
2 tablespoons tomato paste
1 teaspoon dried basil
1 teaspoon dried oregano
1/2 teaspoon garlic power
1/2 teaspoon pepper
1/2 teaspoon salt
20 new potatoes (1 pound) or 3 large Yukon Gold, rough cut
20 baby carrots, or 4 large, rough cut
1 tablespoon olive oil
3 pound leg of lamb, boneless and rolled and tied
1 large sweet onion, thinly sliced
3 tablespoons balsamic vinegar in 3/4 cup warm water

JILL STANFORD

LEMONY LAMB MEATBALLS

These meatballs make a terrific snack (fancy word—hors d'oeuvres) with a cold beverage of choice. Serve with a dish of plain yogurt seasoned with dried dill and a little lemon juice to taste. Provide toothpicks. Or, you can serve these with good cooked noodles dressed in simple olive oil and a teaspoon of oregano, all tossed together.

1 pound ground lamb
1 egg
¼ cup lemon juice, freshly
    squeezed or from a bottle
Peel of 1 lemon, grated
½ teaspoon pepper
½ teaspoon salt
¼ teaspoon garlic salt
1 tablespoon dried parsley
¼ cup plain bread crumbs

1. Preheat the oven to 350°F. Place a sheet of aluminum foil on a baking sheet.

2. Mix the ground lamb with all the other ingredients and shape into golf ball-sized meatballs. (Hint: Wet hands make this a snap.)

3. Place meatballs on the prepared baking sheet and bake about 25 minutes, until they are brown, turning once. Try not to overcook the meatballs, or they become dry.

MAKES 24 SMALL MEATBALLS

RANCH HOUSE-STYLE PORK CHOPS

Our cousin Tommy, who lives in Ohio, has these every single week. And he has since he received the Cowgirl's Cookbook from us quite a few years ago. He likes them that much. You will too!

1. Brown the pork chops in the bacon fat in a heavy skillet. Place a lemon slice on each chop.

2. Mix the ketchup, brown sugar, and water in a small bowl and pour over the chops.

3. Cover the skillet and simmer for 30 minutes, basting the chops occasionally.

SERVES 6

6 pork chops, sliced thick
Bacon fat
6 thin lemon slices
2/3 cup Out of Your Garden Tomato Ketchup (see page 171)
2 tablespoons brown sugar
1/3 cup water

Artificial Oysters

We love oysters, but they are hard to find here in the High Desert of Oregon. And there is always the added dilemma of "Are they fresh?" Well, these will fool you into thinking you are on the briny deep.

Take young green corn and grate it into a bowl until you have a pint. To this add 1 well-beaten egg, a small teacup of flour (about 1/2 cup), 2 or 3 tablespoons of butter, and some salt and pepper, and mix all together. A tablespoonful of the batter is about the size of an oyster. Fry them until light brown, and when they are done, butter them. Don't forget the tartar sauce!

STEAK AND BEANS

It was our good fortune to be introduced to a woman who had cooked real ranch fare nearly all her life. Lila was as tough as some of the steaks she prepared. She shared this recipe, assuring us that this is "the real thing" and that men love it. She said her mother cooked the same thing when she was growing up, but that her mother "didn't have any garlic. I guess I modernized it somewhat."

For the beans
2 cups dried pinto beans
1 tablespoon bacon grease
1 clove garlic, minced
1 medium onion, peeled and
    chopped
½ cup tomato sauce
2 teaspoons Worcestershire
    sauce

For the steak
1 (2-pound) round steak
¼ cup flour, divided
4 tablespoons vegetable oil
Salt and pepper to taste
1 cup whole milk

1. To make the beans, cover the beans with water in a large saucepan and soak for 24 hours.

2. Add the bacon grease to the soaking water. (This will prevent the beans from boiling over.)

3. Add the remaining ingredients. Cook at least 8 to 10 hours over low heat, covered, stirring occasionally. Do not salt while cooking.

4. To make the steak, tenderize the meat by crisscrossing it with a sharp knife, then pounding it with the side of a heavy plate or lid. Roll the tenderized meat in half the flour.

5. Heat the oil in a cast-iron skillet over medium-high heat. Fry the meat in the hot oil for 5 minutes per side. Remove the meat from the pan, place it on an oven-safe platter, and keep it warm in the oven.

6. Sprinkle remaining flour in the drippings in the pan, scraping for the browned bits. Pour in the milk and stir until thickened. Serve the meat with beans on the side.

SERVES 4-6

CHARMAIN MURRAY

WHISKEY-GLAZED PORK LOIN

We can't describe to you how wonderful our kitchen smelled while this was slowly braising in the slow cooker. Just take our word for it. The meat will be tender and flavorful and great for "pulled pork leftovers" the next day. A 4- or 6-quart oval cooker works best.
This dish is delicious served with the Slow Cooker Apple Butter found on page 158, baked and mashed squash, and an apple vinaigrette salad.

1. Spray the inside of a slow cooker with cooking spray. Place the apple and onion pieces in the bottom of the pot, then lay the meat on top.

2. Combine the next five ingredients in a bowl and pour over the meat. Sprinkle the red pepper flakes, salt, and pepper over the top.

3. Cook on high for 4 hours or low for 6 to 8 hours, or until the meat thermometer registers 145°F when inserted into the thickest part of the meat.

SERVES 4-6

2 large Granny Smith apples, cored and cut into 8 pieces lengthwise
1 white onion, peeled and cut into lengthwise slices
2 pounds boneless pork loin, or 6 boneless pork chops
1/4 cup brown sugar
1 teaspoon ground ginger
1/2 cup Pendleton Whisky (or substitute soy sauce)
1/4 cup ketchup
10 peppercorns
2 tablespoons red pepper flakes
Salt and pepper to taste

For this picture, we used half of the pork loin and one apple, no onion. The other half is in the freezer for another day.

JILL STANFORD

WILD GAME

ELK HEART AND LIVER

Caprice Madison lives up in the Flattops Wilderness in Colorado. She has a Facebook page called "Mountain Woman." Curious, we "friended" her. She said she was going out hunting, and we asked if she would share a recipe with us. She replied, "My husband and I hunt here in Colorado. The game meat we get sustains us through winter. This is a great favorite when we get back to the cabin."

She went on: "My husband guided a hunter for a bull elk this year. The first day he shot too high. Then the next day my husband took him to a place to 'stand' and the hunter said, 'I can't walk that far.' The next day (this went on for seven days) they rode out, and again my husband had him in some elk—about fourteen—but the hunter didn't see them, so my husband said, 'Well, why don't we just go scatter 'em?' On another day he missed his shot and my husband said, 'Reload!' but the hunter said, 'I don't have my ammo with me, it's on my horse.' FINALLY on the last day his hunter got a bull! We ate the heart and liver. Instead of saying 'Pass the salt and pepper' up here, it's 'Pass the ammo.'"

1 fresh elk heart, washed
1 fresh elk liver, washed and
   peeled

1. Cut 'em up.

2. Soak 'em in salt water for a day or two.

3. Roll 'em in flour with salt and pepper to taste and fry 'em up.

SERVES 2–4

FAMILY MINCEMEAT PIE FILLING

Our cousin Bob Stanford sent this to us. Since our families always met for Thanksgiving when we were younger, we remember this mincemeat pie his mother, Aunt Louise Stanford, would make.

"While talking with my cousin Jill about her new book, the thought came to me of my Grandmother and her mother, Great Grandma Woods, and their tradition in the fall of making and canning mincemeat pie filling. This tradition started in Sisters, Oregon, in Great Grandma's ranch kitchen more than 100 years ago. My mother, Louise Stanford, was the last to make this treasured family recipe for mincemeat. Sadly, they are all gone, but the memory of Grandpa boning the meat and the rest of the women putting the ingredients together is very clear to me. The venison is the foundation for this recipe. Carl and Maud Woods would be proud and pleased for some of you to carry this recipe on. This recipe reads exactly from Grandma's handwritten recipe. I don't know the size of the 'bowl.' However, I believe it to be about 1 cup."

Cook all the ingredients together until the apples are tender. Put in sterilized jars and seal well.

- 3 bowls venison meat
- 5 bowls apples
- 1 bowl molasses
- 1 bowl vinegar
- 1 bowl suet
- 3 bowls raisins
- 5 bowls sugar
- 2 bowls orange juice pulp
- 2 tablespoons nutmeg
- 2 tablespoons cloves
- 2 tablespoons cinnamon
- 2 tablespoons black pepper
- 2 tablespoons salt
- 3 lemons run through the food chopper, peel and all

BUTTERMILK FRIED RABBIT

Denice Casey lives in Pritchett, Colorado, where she raises registered quarter horses. (And they are gorgeous!) She captured and trained a red tail hawk she has named Shikoba. She says, "I am a second season apprentice falconer. After this season, I will become a general falconer." It's been a long, hard, and often painful journey for them both. (Those talons and his beak are sharp!) All that work and patience has paid off. Shikoba trusts Denice and will hunt for her. He often catches the jack rabbits that are plentiful on Denice's land, which she skins and puts in her freezer all cleaned and cut into pieces for a stew or a fry later. We will let her tell you how she prepares this dish:

"If you are using wild cottontails, I highly recommend you brine your rabbits before frying. A simple brine of 1/4 cup kosher salt to 4 cups water will do—the rabbit is going to get plenty of seasoning later. Submerge the rabbit in this brine for up to 12 hours. This process keeps them moist. Domesticated rabbits don't really need this, but if you want to brine them, do so for no more than 4 hours.

As a general rule, 1 domestic rabbit will serve two to three people, as will a jackrabbit. A snowshoe hare will serve two, a cottontail and a squirrel just one. You can also do this with chicken (of course), as well as quail.

2 cups buttermilk
2 tablespoons Italian
seasoning, or mix together
1½ teaspoons oregano, 1½
2 to teaspoons thyme, and
1 tablespoon dried parsley
1 tablespoon paprika

1 tablespoon garlic powder
2 teaspoons cayenne, or to taste
4 cottontail rabbits, cut into serving pieces
1½ cups flour
1 heaping teaspoon salt
2 cups vegetable oil for frying

1. Mix the buttermilk with the all the spices except the salt and flour. Coat the rabbit with the mixture and set in a covered container overnight, or at least 8 hours.

2. When you are ready to fry, pour the oil into a large pan—a big cast-iron frying pan is ideal—to a depth of about an inch. The general idea is you want the oil to come halfway up the side of the rabbit. Set the heat to medium-high.

3. Meanwhile, take the rabbit out of the buttermilk and let it drain in a colander. Don't shake off the buttermilk or anything, just leave it there.

4. Let the oil heat until it is about 325°F; this is the point where a sprinkle of flour will immediately sizzle. When the oil is hot, pour the flour and salt into a plastic bag and shake to combine. Put a few pieces of rabbit into the bag and shake to get them coated in flour.

5. Set the coated rabbit pieces in one layer in the hot oil so they don't touch. Fry for about 8 to 12 minutes. Fry gently—you want a steady sizzle, but nothing raging, and you definitely don't want the rabbit to just sit in the oil. You might need to adjust the heat. Turn the rabbit pieces and fry for another 10 minutes or so, until they are golden brown. The forelegs will come out first, followed by the loin, and the hind legs will come out last. You will probably need to fry in batches, so just leave the uncooked rabbit pieces in the colander until you are ready to flour them up and fry them. Don't let the floured pieces sit.

6. When the rabbit pieces are good and fried, let them rest on a rack set over a paper towel to drain away any excess oil. If you are cooking in batches, set this in a warm oven.

7. Serve fried rabbit with grits, potato salad, coleslaw, or really whatever. Oh, and should you have leftovers, they are fantastic cold for lunch the next day.

SERVES 4

Blanche McGoughey   Bertha Blancett   Dolly Mullins

HONEY OF A PHEASANT DISH

Our friend Peter Voorhies was an avid bird hunter but had no wife to cook the pheasants and ducks (and the occasional goose) he bagged. Our deal was he would provide the birds and a bottle of wine, and we would cook the meal. The only problem was we had no idea how to cook game. We learned fast! Pheasant is a favorite of ours now, but we learned the hard way that it is a very dry bird with precious little fat on it.

1. Preheat the oven to 400°F. Put the pheasants in a small baking dish (Pheasant are not very large!).

2. Spread honey over each bird, including the legs, thighs, and wings. Pour the lemon juice over the pheasants. Season the cavities generously with salt, pepper, and half a lemon each. Season the skin with salt, pepper, garlic powder, and the thyme. Lay a bacon strip lengthwise over each bird.

3. Put the baking dish in the oven on the second shelf up from the bottom. Bake until the bacon is cooked and a leg of a pheasant will move easily. Try not to overcook these birds.

SERVES 2

2 pheasants, cleaned and dressed (Be sure to check for shot—they can break a tooth.)
Enough honey to cover both birds
1/4 cup lemon juice
Salt and pepper
1 lemon, halved
Garlic powder to taste
1/2 teaspoon thyme (1/4 teaspoon per bird)
2 slices bacon, one for each bird

JILL'S WILD DUCK

Many years ago, Jill's husband had a friend who hunted wild duck every weekend during the season. He and his faithful spaniel would go out at dawn and bring me the ducks by mid-afternoon. He would be back at 6 p.m. for dinner. She tried many recipes, often complicated. This one was the best as well as the easiest.

4 small ducks, cleaned and checked for buckshot
4 cups peeled and coarsely chopped potatoes
2 cups coarsely chopped carrots
1 medium onion, coarsely chopped
1 package onion soup mix
2 tablespoons butter, cut into rough pieces
Salt and pepper to taste
Bacon (optional)

1. Preheat the oven to 325°F. Wash the ducks and wipe them dry inside and out. Fold their wings behind them and tie their legs together.

2. Place all the vegetables in a Dutch oven with 1/2 cup water. Place the ducks on top of the vegetables. Sprinkle the soup mix over them, then drop in the butter all over them. Cover.

3. Bake the ducks for about 20 to 25 minutes, or until tender. Uncover and roast for about 5 to 10 minutes more to brown the skin. Be careful not to overbake these wild duck; they are dry to begin with. If you like you can put a half slice of bacon over each breast to help keep them moist.

4. These are best served with a wild rice mix and a salad with a sharp vinaigrette dressing.

SERVES 4

SLOW COOKER VENISON

 The word venison means "meat from a deer." It comes to us from Middle English that began as the Old French venesoun, which can be traced all the way back to the Latin venatio, or "hunting." All of this goes to show that we have been consuming "meat from a deer" for a very long time.

1. In a slow cooker or deep and heavy casserole dish with a lid, add the soup, wine (if using), bouillon, garlic, onion, mushrooms, Tabasco, and thyme. Stir to mix well.

2. Add the roast to the pot. Turn it several times to coat. Turn the slow cooker on high and cook 4 to 6 hours, or until the meat is just tender.

3. Cook the potatoes and carrots in boiling salted water until fork-tender. Drain.

4. Take the roast out of the slow cooker and place it on a platter. If making gravy for the roast, put the starch in a cup, add the water, and stir it with a fork. Whisk this into the hot liquid in the slow cooker. Stir until gravy thickens.

5. Serve the roast with potatoes and carrots, if desired, or with cooked egg noodles or brown rice.

SERVES 8

1 (10½-ounce) can cream of mushroom soup, undiluted

1 cup Cabernet Sauvignon or dry red wine (optional)

2 beef bouillon cubes, crumbled

3 cloves garlic, peeled and minced

1 large onion, diced

1 (8-ounce) can sliced mushrooms, drained

1 tablespoon Tabasco sauce

2 teaspoons thyme, crumbled

3 pounds venison roast (or lean beef roast if the hunt didn't go so well)

6 large potatoes, quartered

8 carrots, peeled and cut into 4-inch pieces (optional)

3–4 tablespoons cornstarch (optional)

¼ cup water (optional)

WILD HOG MEATBALLS

Audrey Clossen lives in Spring Branch, Texas. When we asked her if she was a cowgirl, she replied, "I am a cowgirl in spirit only, although I DO have 'Should've Been a Cowboy' by Toby Keith for a ringtone on my phone. I run back and forth from the Hill Country to the beautiful Gulf of Mexico and the islands there. Sometimes we really DO wear cowboy boots!" That works for us! No wild hog handy? Use ground pork from the grocery store. These meatballs are simply out of this world.

For the meatballs
2 cups bread crumbs
1/2 cup milk
1 pound finely ground wild
    pork (or market pork)
1 pound finely ground beef
3 eggs
1 cup chopped yellow onions
1–2 tablespoons ground
    cardamom
Salt and pepper to taste
1/2 cup (1 stick) butter, divided
6 cups sliced yellow onions
1/2 cup sugar
1 sprig parsley

1. To prepare the meatballs, soak the bread crumbs in the milk in a large mixing bowl for 5 minutes. Mix in the meat, eggs, and chopped onions. Season with cardamom and salt and pepper to taste. Roll into 1- to 1½-inch meatballs.

2. Melt ¼ cup butter in a skillet and sauté the meatballs for approximately 20 minutes.

3. In a separate skillet, sauté the sliced onions with ¼ cup butter and sugar until caramelized, about 10 to 15 minutes. Season with salt and pepper to taste.

4. Remove the meatballs and the onions from both pans and place on separate plates.

5. To make the gravy, deglaze both sauté pans with the ½ cup butter and the beef broth, scraping up the browned bits. Cook over high heat for 1 minute.

6. Place the contents of both pans into one large pot, and stir in the cream and caramelized onions. Season with nutmeg, allspice, cinnamon, and cloves. Bring to a simmer.

7. Mix the cornstarch and water together. With a whisk, mix this slurry into the cream sauce. Add the meatballs and simmer approximately 20 to 30 minutes.

8. Serve meatballs on top of egg noodles or a slice of bread and garnish with parsley.

SERVES 6

For the gravy

½ cup (1 stick) butter
3 cups beef broth
2 cups heavy cream
1 teaspoon ground nutmeg
1 teaspoon ground allspice
¼ teaspoon cinnamon
¼ teaspoon cloves
3½ tablespoons cornstarch
¼ cup water

JILL STANFORD

RELISHES, JAMS, JELLIES, SALSAS, AND SAUCES

SLOW COOKER APPLE BUTTER

The smell of apples really means fall to us. Apple pie, applesauce, and apple butter are fall favorites. This slow cooker apple butter is rich, thick, and sweet. Put it on a piece of toast or a toasted English muffin. Served over the Whiskey-Glazed Pork Loin on page 143, this is just about perfect. Best of all? It's fat free! Your chinks will still fit.

5½ pounds apples, or 10 cups, peeled, cored, and chopped small

½ cup honey

1 cup brown sugar

1 tablespoon ground cinnamon

¼ teaspoon ground cloves

¼ teaspoon ground ginger

¼ teaspoon salt

¼ cup apple cider

1. Place the prepared apples in a slow cooker that has been sprayed with nonstick spray.

2. In a medium bowl, mix the honey, brown sugar, spices, and salt. Pour the mixture over the apples in the slow cooker and mix well.

3. Pour the apple cider over all and mix once more. Cover and cook on high 1 hour.

4. Reduce heat to low and cook 9 to 11 hours more, stirring occasionally, until the mixture is thickened and dark brown. Uncover and continue cooking on low for 1 more hour. Stir with a whisk to increase smoothness. Add more cider if it is becoming dry.

5. Spoon the mixture into sterile containers, cover, and refrigerate or freeze.

MAKES 7–8 PINTS

Note: If you want to make this on the stovetop: combine everything into a large casserole that has a lid; mix well. Cover and cook over medium-high heat for 1 hour, or until the apples are tender, stirring occasionally. With the lid off, continue to cook on medium to low heat for 30 minutes, or until the apple butter is thick.

JILL STANFORD

BERTHA BLANCETT'S QUINCE JELLY

Quince is a golden or greenish yellow fruit. Hard and shaped like an apple, it grows on a small, thorny bush related to the rose family. The five-petal flowers range from deep red to pale salmon. Because it is so hardy, the quince bush is always a staple in pioneer homesteads.

1. Scrub and cut quince into quarters. Remove the seeds. Place in a sauce-pan and add enough water to cover the fruit. Cover the pan and cook until soft. Drain, then force through a sieve.

2. To 3 cups of quince pulp, add sugar. Cook until thick and smooth, about 20 minutes. Stir frequently, as it will want to stick.

3. Put into hot, sterilized jars.

MAKES 3 CUPS

6 quince
3–4 cups sugar

Bertha Blancett

Bertha Kaepernick Blancett was the quintessential cowgirl. As a young girl she would ride her saddle horse over the hills to the local rodeos, leading her bucking horse. She'd climb aboard and ride it out to the whistle. She competed against men, and she nearly always took home the prize money.

An All-Around Cowgirl at the Pendleton Round-Up from 1911 to 1918, Bertha won the cowgirls' bucking contest many times, as well as trick-riding and relay-racing contests.

Bertha married a cowboy named Del. Her German heritage never left her, and she was as adept in the kitchen as she was in the corrals.

In 1999 Bertha was inducted into the National Cowgirl Hall of Fame due to the efforts of my friend Joanna Stewart, herself a cowgirl and daughter of Andy Her-regia, noted stock contractor. Bertha lived her last years on the Herregia Ranch in Southern California, and Stewart followed her around and learned quite a few things, including how to make this unusual jelly. I am proud to have been part of the effort to induct Bertha into the Pendleton Round-Up Hall of Fame and to have delivered her trunk and clothes to the Museum.

Bertha Blancett
AUTHOR'S COLLECTION

EASY STRAWBERRY FREEZER JAM

It is the dead of winter—cold and dreary. What could be nicer than bright, fresh, and delicious strawberry jam on your toast before you head out to feed the livestock? But wait! You didn't pick any strawberries in the summer. Store-bought frozen strawberries to the rescue!

4 cups (dry measure) fresh or frozen strawberries
4 cups sugar
1 (1.75-ounce) packet of fruit pectin (Sure-Jell)
3/4 cup water

1. Wash the strawberries if fresh; thaw if frozen.

2. In a large bowl, mash the strawberries with a potato masher. Add the sugar and stir well. Let the strawberries sit for 15 to 30 minutes, stirring every once in a while to make sure the sugar dissolves. Set aside.

3. Sprinkle the pectin in a small saucepan and add the water. Stir well until the pectin is completely dissolved. Then place the saucepan over high heat and bring the mixture to a boil; let it boil hard for at least 1 minute.

4. Immediately pour the hot pectin into the strawberry mixture and mix well. Keep stirring for another 3 or 4 minutes.

5. Ladle the jam into clean jars or plastic containers (make sure the jam is cool enough for plastic), cover with lids, and label. Let the jars sit out overnight to jell completely, then store in the freezer. But first, make a piece of toast . . .

MAKES 5 CUPS

ROBIN JOHNSON

ROBIN'S PICKLED RED AND SWEET ONIONS

These are a wonderful accompaniment to hamburgers, and they are easy to make. They also make a great "Gift from My Garden" with some raffia tied around the lids.

1. Tightly pack the onions into a clean glass canning jar.

2. In a saucepan, combine the vinegar, water, spices, and sugar; bring to a boil over medium heat and cook about 5 minutes, stirring once or twice.

ROBIN JOHNSON

3. Pour the hot liquid over the onions in the jars. Let them cool on the counter.

When cool, put sterilized lids on the jars, tighten, and store in the refrigerator for a day.

4. The next day, carefully drain the liquid into a saucepan, bring it to a boil, and then pour it—again—over the onions.

5. Cool, cover again, and let the onions sit in the refrigerator overnight. Then repeat this process one more time the next day. The onions are ready when they are again chilled. Keep the pickled onions in the refrigerator, and they will be good for 3 or 4 months.

MAKES 2 QUARTS OR 4 PINT JARS

2½ cups sweet and red onions (1½ cups sweet onions, such as Walla Walla or Vidalia, 1 cup red onions), cut in ⅛-inch-thick half rings
½ cup white or wine vinegar
½ cup cold water
1 tablespoon pickling spices (see below)
1 cup white sugar

Pickling spices are available already combined and labeled as such in the spice section of the grocery store.

Or, you can make your own: Combine 1 tablespoon mustard seed, 2 teaspoons whole allspice, 1 teaspoon coriander or caraway seeds, ¼ teaspoon red pepper flakes (or more if you like it hot!), ½ teaspoon ground ginger, 1 bay leaf (broken into pieces), ½ cinnamon stick (broken into pieces), and 4 whole cloves.

Other good flavorings for your pickling spice include celery seed, dill seeds and/or sprigs, fennel seeds, whole peppercorns, whole or sliced garlic cloves, fresh oregano leaves, and mustard seed.

TRICK RIDERS' ORANGE AND CRANBERRY SAUCE

Peggy Veach-Robinson is the daughter of Monroe Veach, maker of the best trick-riding saddles. Peggy herself was a trick rider in her younger days. Today she runs the saddle shop in Trenton, Missouri, where they not only make trick saddles, but all kinds and styles of Western saddles. Here is a neat "trick" from Peggy for your next Thanksgiving.

1 (11-ounce) can mandarin oranges
1 (12-ounce) package fresh or frozen cranberries
3/4 cup sugar
1 teaspoon ground ginger
1/2 cup chopped pecans

1. Drain the oranges, but reserve 1/4 cup of the syrup.

2. In a medium-size microwave-safe bowl, microwave the cranberries, sugar, and ginger in the reserved orange syrup on high for 7 to 11 minutes, or until the cranberries pop.

3. Stir in the oranges and pecans. Chill and serve.

SERVES 6-8

JILL STANFORD

MARGUERITE'S MARINARA SAUCE

Our mother Marguerite was an inventive cook. She would never run out of ideas, and the people who got to partake of her imagination—including us—just loved everything she cooked. This was a favorite for family and guests alike.

1. In a large saucepan, sauté the diced onion until it starts to brown slightly. Add the garlic and cook for 2 minutes.

2. Add the spaghetti sauce mix and then the wine, water, and pasta sauce. Mix well.

3. Bring this to just boiling and then turn down and simmer slowly, lid off, for about an hour. If it starts to get too thick, add another 1/4 cup water.

4. Enjoy over your favorite pasta.

SERVES 4-6

Note: You can add a pound of cooked hamburger or sausage to make it a meat sauce.

1 onion (diced)
2 or 3 cloves garlic, minced
1 package spaghetti sauce mix
1 cup red or white wine
1/2 cup water
1 (24-ounce) jar pasta sauce

ROBIN JOHNSON

COFFEE BEAN STEAK RUB

High-octane good!

1 tablespoon whole coffee
    beans
1 tablespoon white
    peppercorns
⅛ teaspoon paprika
½ tablespoon garlic powder
½ tablespoon sea salt
1 tablespoon all-purpose
    seasoning

1. Combine all the ingredients in a blender or spice or coffee grinder and finely grind the mixture.

2. Rub onto your favorite steak or tri-tip 30 minutes or more prior to cooking.

MAKES 1 RUB, OR ¼ CUP

Cowgirl is an attitude, really. A pioneer spirit, a special American brand of courage. The cowgirl faces life head on, lives by her own lights, and makes no excuses. Cowgirls take stands. They speak up. They defend the things they hold dear. A cowgirl might be a rancher, or a barrel racer, or a bull rider, or an actress. But she's just as likely to be a checker at the local Winn Dixie, a full-time mother, a banker, an attorney, or an astronaut.

—Dale Evans Rogers, "The Queen of the Cowgirls," Los Angeles, 1992

COWGIRL CRUDE SALSA

For those of you who insist that it isn't Western if there isn't a salsa, here's your salsa. Cowgirls don't have a lot of time to spend fussing, so a "crude" (meaning "roughly chopped") tomato hot sauce salsa has a clean and fresh taste. Depending on the amount and kind of peppers and chiles you use, the intensity of hotness can range from mild to volcanic. This Texas-style salsa tastes best at room temperature, so take it out of the fridge at least an hour before you use it for dipping corn chips, as a topping for frittatas, or as a condiment with any Mexican entree. Olé!

Combine all the ingredients. Refrigerate until at least 1 hour before serving. Store in the refrigerator for up to 1 week.

MAKES ABOUT 2 CUPS

3 ripe tomatoes, chopped
1/4–1/2 cup minced hot
    peppers (fresh or canned)
1/2 cup finely chopped onion
Tabasco or other hot sauce
    to taste
Salt and pepper to taste
3/4 cup chopped Spanish
    olives (optional)

JILL STANFORD

COWGIRL'S HOMEMADE TOMATO SAUCE

We went to a farmers' market and bought a lot of organic Roma tomatoes. A lot. We went back to Robin's place and peeled and chopped and canned them for hours. The result was a bounty of pint-size glass jars filled with wonderful bright-red tomatoes just asking to have things happen to them all winter long. Here is what we did with 8 small Roma tomatoes that didn't go into a jar.

1 tablespoon butter
8 small Roma tomatoes, peeled and diced
1/4 cup chopped fresh or 2 tablespoons dried basil
1 teaspoon olive oil
1 teaspoon garlic salt
Salt and freshly ground black pepper to taste
1 tablespoon all-purpose flour
1/4 cup water
1 clove garlic, diced

1. Melt the butter in a large skillet over medium heat. Cook the tomatoes in the melted butter until they begin to fall apart, about 5 to 7 minutes. (If you use your own home-canned tomatoes, or a can of whole tomatoes, just heat them in the butter.)

2. Add the basil, olive oil, garlic salt, salt, and pepper.

3. Slowly stir the flour into the mixture and cook until it begins to thicken, about 5 to 7 minutes.

4. Stir the water through the mixture to break up any lumps of flour. Mix the garlic into the sauce and simmer another 5 minutes.

5. Serve hot over any pasta.

SERVES 2

GREEN TOMATO RELISH

A rainy summer can mean only one thing—green tomatoes. There are some of us who relish (get it?) green tomatoes. Here's how.

1. Combine all the ingredients in a heavy pot and cook slowly, stirring often, until the relish reaches a good, thick consistency.

2. Pack the relish into sterile 8-ounce canning jars and seal. Process in a hot water bath for 25 minutes.

MAKES ABOUT 10 (8-OUNCE) JARS FOR THE PANTRY

18 cups green tomatoes, diced and drained
2 large Walla Walla sweet onions, chopped fine
1 red pepper, seeded and chopped fine
1 green pepper, seeded and chopped fine
3 cups vinegar
9 cups sugar
3 tablespoons coarse salt
1 teaspoon allspice
1 teaspoon cloves
2 tablespoons cinnamon
2 tablespoons nutmeg

There are 2 theories to arguing with a woman . . . neither works.

—Will Rogers

Keepin' It Simple Barbeque Sauce

The cowgirl most responsible for bringing back to life the cowgirls of the past is Polly Helm, originally from Pendleton, Oregon, home of the world-famous Pendleton Round-Up. She discovered a photo of Kitty Canutt (titled "Champion of All") and started collecting other images and information of "lady buckaroos." In 1986 she put it all together in the form of the Pendleton Cowgirl Company, which produces calendars, note cards, magnets, and more that feature an old print on the front and its story on the back.

Polly says, "The cowgirl spirit is a state of mind and heart. The mystique is built around the idea of women doing what they love to do, despite the risks involved. It's about being true to oneself."

Her recipe for barbecue sauce is simple. Here it is in her words: "Equal parts ketchup, mustard, dark molasses, and Worcestershire sauce. Nothin' fancy, but always a favorite at our annual summer rib fest."

SOME LIKE IT HOT SAUCE

A word of caution: Jalapeños have 2,500 to 8,000 Scoville units. The Scoville scale measures the "spicy heat" of chile peppers. Compared to other chiles, the jalapeño has a heat level that varies from mild to hot depending on cultivation and preparation. Some people wear latex or vinyl gloves while cutting, skinning, or seeding jalapeños. When preparing jalapeños, your hands should not come in contact with your eyes, as this causes painful burning and redness. Jalapeño juice is often used as a remedy for seasonal allergies and cardiovascular problems.

All that being said, warnings issued, this is a great hot sauce that will blow your boots off.

1. In a medium glass or enamel-lined saucepan—not stainless steel or aluminum—over high heat, combine oil, peppers, garlic, onion, and salt; sauté for 4 minutes.

2. Add the water and cook for 20 minutes, stirring often. Remove from heat and allow the sauce to cool to room temperature.

3. Transfer the sauce to a food processor or blender and puree until smooth. With the processor or the blender running, slowly add the vinegar.

4. Pour into a sterilized 1 quart canning jar with a tight lid. Keep refrigerated.

MAKES 4 CUPS

1 teaspoon vegetable oil
18 fresh jalapeño peppers, sliced and seeded
3 garlic cloves, minced
1 cup sweet onion, minced
3/4 teaspoon salt
2 cups water
1 cup distilled white vinegar

SUMMERTIME OR ANYTIME PEACH SALSA

We love peach salsa! You can dip tortilla chips in it, of course, but how about serving it on pancakes or waffles in the middle of winter? That will start your day off right! When you are chopping jalapeños, remove the seeds and veins from the peppers and always wear gloves to avoid mistakenly rubbing your eyes and owwww! If you want salsa with a lot of heat, then leave the seeds in.

Half-pint jars of salsa wrapped with a little red raffia make great gifts.

6 ripe peaches, peeled, pitted, and diced
1/2 cup white vinegar
1 1/4 cups chopped sweet onion
4 jalapeño peppers, chopped
1 red bell pepper, seeded and chopped
1/2 cup finely chopped, loosely packed cilantro
2 tablespoons honey
1 clove garlic, peeled and finely chopped
1 1/2 teaspoons cumin
1/2 teaspoon cayenne pepper

1. Combine all the ingredients in a saucepan and bring to a boil over medium heat, stirring the entire time so it does not scorch. Reduce the heat and continue boiling gently until the salsa is slightly thickened.

2. Ladle the hot salsa mix into 4 pint or 8 half-pint washed and sterilized jars. Leave a little room on top for expansion.

3. Wipe the jar rims and then tighten on the lids. Put the filled jars in a large pot filled with water that has been brought to a boil and then allowed to simmer. Be sure the jars are completely covered. Bring the water back to a boil and process the salsa for 15 minutes.

4. Remove the jars and place them on a folded dish towel on the counter to cool completely. Then listen for the "ping" of each successfully sealed jar when you tap on the top of the lid.

MAKES 4 PINT OR 8 HALF-PINT JARS OF HOT STUFF!

OUT OF YOUR GARDEN TOMATO KETCHUP

No need to travel down the road to the store for this one staple every cowgirl should have in her pantry!

Crush the tomatoes through a sieve directly into a large saucepan. Add the rest of the ingredients and cook slowly until desired thickness. Place into hot, sterilized jars and seal.

MAKES 2–3 PINTS

1 gallon tomatoes, peeled and chopped (about 16 tomatoes)
1 quart white vinegar
1 quart white sugar
1/2 teaspoon red pepper flakes
1 teaspoon allspice
1/2 teaspoon black pepper
1 tablespoon salt

Cowgirls have three main dishes: meats, vegetables, and breads. They use three spices: salt, pepper, and catsup.

—Anonymous

DESSERTS AND SWEETS

ANGEL CAKE

This is so easy we are almost embarrassed to include it. That being said, the key word is easy. Isn't that what cowgirls like?

1 box angel food cake mix (dry)

1 (20–22-ounce) fruit pie filling, any flavor (We liked the blueberry.)

1. In an ungreased 9 x 13-inch pan, mix together the angel food cake mix and the pie filling. Full disclosure: This is the hard part. The dry mix and the sticky filling take a little work to fully mix. We used a fork. Be sure to get into the corners of the pan.

2. Bake at 350°F for 28 to 30 minutes. It will puff up all by itself and look attractive! That's it!

3. Serve while still warm, topped with vanilla ice cream (which you can make and found on page 176) or whipped cream.

SERVES 4-6

JILL STANFORD

BA'S BIRTHDAY CARROT CAKE WITH BOURBON CREAM CHEESE FROSTING

Jill has been making this carrot cake for her best friend for twenty years. Moist and rich, it's the best birthday—or any special occasion—cake you can make. We sent this off to Cowgirl Charmain Murray to kitchen-test and you can see the results. She loved it too!

1. To make the cake, preheat the oven to 350°F. Grease and flour 2 8-inch round cake pans. Line the bottoms with a round of greased parchment paper.

2. Beat the eggs and sugar together until creamy. Add the vegetable oil, slowly and continue to beat.

3. Sift together the dry ingredients, then add them to the egg mixture, beating well.

4. Add the vanilla and bourbon, if using. Then add the carrots and raisins.

5. Pour the batter into the prepared cake pans, level the mixture, and bake for 25 to 30 minutes. Remove cakes from the pans, and when they are cool, frost with Bourbon Cream Cheese Frosting.

CHARMAIN MURRAY

For the cake
2 cups sugar
4 eggs
1 cup vegetable oil
2½ cups white flour
2 teaspoons baking soda
2 teaspoons cinnamon
½ teaspoon salt
2 teaspoons vanilla
3 tablespoons bourbon whiskey (optional)
3 cups grated carrots
½ cup golden raisins

For the frosting
1 (8-ounce) package cream cheese, softened
½ cup (1 stick) butter, softened
2 tablespoons bourbon
1 teaspoon vanilla extract
2 cups sifted powdered sugar
1 tablespoon chopped walnuts, toasted (optional) to garnish the top

COWGIRLS EZ ICE CREAM

How about this? Ice cream without a churn? Ice cream any time you want? We'd say this is pretty wonderful. You will too.

For variations, you can cut caramel squares into quarters (use wet scissor blades or a knife that is wet) and fold these pieces into the finished ice cream before freezing. Top with sea salt. Pieces of your favorite chocolate, chopped, is a great addition too. We chopped up peppermint bark!

1 (14-ounce) can sweetened condensed milk
1 teaspoon vanilla
2 cups very cold whipping cream
Coarse sea salt (optional)

1. Take the label off the sweetened condensed milk and put the can, unopened, in a medium pot filled with boiling water. Turn down the heat to low or simmer. The can should be completely submerged, standing up. Cover the pan and let the can simmer for 2 hours and then remove the can from the water (use tongs!) and let it cool.

2. Open the can and pour the thickened milk into a large bowl. It will pour very slowly because it has thickened to caramel in its bath. (The very fancy term for this is dulce de leche, which is Spanish for "caramel." Impress your friends!)

3. Stir in the vanilla and let it cool a little more, at least 10 minutes.

4. Beat the cold whipped cream with an electric mixer in another large bowl until very stiff peaks form, about 3 minutes.

5. Stir about a third of the whipped cream into the caramel until just combined. Gently fold the remaining whipped cream into the caramel and pour into 9 x 5-inch loaf pan. Cover with plastic wrap and freeze until firm, about 6 hours.

6. Before serving, sprinkle a bit of coarse sea salt on the top for a "fancy" presentation.

Note: This ice cream can be made up to seven days ahead of time. Just keep it covered and frozen.

MAKES ABOUT 5 SERVINGS. OR ONE.

JILL STANFORD

Cowgirl's Never-Fail Pie Crust

2 cups all-purpose flour
1 teaspoon sugar
1 teaspoon salt
2/3 cup canola oil
6 tablespoons ice water

1. Mix together the flour, sugar and salt, then add the oil and water. Mix well.

2. Divide the dough in half and roll each piece between two pieces of plastic wrap.

We knooooow! It really, really works. Easy-peasey, flaky and fast!

COWGIRLS XO CHOCOLATE SAUCE

This yummy sauce can be stored in the refrigerator for a month. However, it does thicken in the refrigerator and will need to be heated slightly to get it to pour again.

1/4 cup butter
8 pieces or 1/2 package
    Unsweetened Baking
    Chocolate
1/2 cup light corn syrup
11/2 cups sugar
1/4 to 1/2 cup hot water

1. Melt the butter and chocolate together over medium heat in a small saucepan, stirring constantly. When melted, add the corn syrup and sugar and then add about 1/4 to 1/2 cup hot water and continue to stir constantly. Stir and cook slowly until the mixture is smooth and the sauce coats the back of the spoon well (about 5 minutes).

2. Serve as hot fudge sauce or allow to cool and serve cold over ice cream and cake.

MAKES ABOUT 11/2 CUPS

FANCY MINTS

Even cowgirls now and then have to come up with something for a wedding, shower, or birthday celebration. These mints are easy, good to eat, and fancy!

1. Cream the butter in a large mixing bowl and then add the powdered sugar ½ cup at a time, reserving ⅛ cup of the powdered sugar for dipping.

2. Add the heavy cream slowly and beat thoroughly after each addition.

3. Add oil of peppermint or peppermint extract, one drop at a time, to taste.

4. Divide the mixture into however many colors you wish for your fancy mints. Select a color and add one scant drop of the coloring until you reach the color you want. For a pale pink, add a small amount of red; yellow for buttercup yellow; yellow and green for mint color; and a tiny amount of blue for sky blue.

5. Roll the mints into small balls, place on parchment paper, and press with a fork that has been dipped in powdered sugar. Let set overnight.

MAKES ABOUT 36 CANDIES

½ pound butter
1 (16-ounce) package powdered sugar, divided
1 tablespoon heavy cream
Oil of peppermint or peppermint extract to taste
Food coloring

ROBIN JOHNSON

HAZEL DUNCAN'S GINGERBREAD

Our friend Mary Lynn Duncan submitted this to us, along with a picture that we could almost taste because it looked so good.

3 cups flour (preferably Gold Medal brand)

1 teaspoon ground ginger

1 teaspoon ground cinnamon

1 teaspoon ground cloves

1 teaspoon salt

1/4 teaspoon baking soda

2 3/4 teaspoons baking powder

1/2 cup shortening or softened butter

1/2 cup sugar

2 eggs

1 cup molasses

3/4 cup hot water

1. Preheat the oven to 350°F and grease a pan, preferably an interesting one*.

2. Sift together the dry ingredients in a medium bowl.

3. Cream together the shortening or butter, sugar, eggs, and molasses in a large bowl.

4. Add the dry mixture alternately with the hot water to the creamed mixture, blending well after each addition. Pour into prepared pan and bake for 1 hour.

5. Serve as is or with whipped cream or vanilla ice cream or with Butter-cream Frosting (page 181) on top.

Note: The "interesting pan" used is a Bundt cake pan. Good choice!

MARY LYNN DUNCAN

BUTTERCREAM FROSTING

Blend together the butter, cream, and vanilla extract and then begin adding the powdered sugar, a little at a time, blending thoroughly with each addition.

MAKES ENOUGH TO FROST TWO 8- TO 9-INCH LAYERS OR A MESS OF COOKIES

6 tablespoons butter, softened
1/4 cup light cream
1 1/2 teaspoons pure vanilla extract
4 3/4 cups powdered sugar

Hazel Marie Jones Padgitt Duncan

Hazel Marie Jones Padgitt Duncan was born in Donalda, Alberta, Canada on St. Patrick's Day in 1912. She came to America with her parents, Fred and Della Marie Jones, along with two sisters and two brothers, in about 1918 by covered wagon. Eventually the family settled in Ephrata, Washington, where Fred set up his business, a blacksmith shop. The family homesteaded there, and eventually another brother was born.

Hazel attended school there, graduated from high school, married Charlie Padgitt, and was a momma to five daughters and one son. She lost her beloved husband Charlie to lung cancer. A few years later she met and fell in love with my dad, Jesse E. Duncan, newly retired from thirty years in the Navy. They married, and a couple of years later, I was born, much loved and wanted by my parents and older siblings. They all tell me (even my sisters and brother) that I was born horse crazy, much to the delight of my folks, who were both raised with horses. By the time I came along in 1957, they had a little more money and a lot more time to indulge a kid (that was me!), and they both loved that all I ever really thought about was horses.

Mom was a real cowgirl, too. She loved horses and knew how to work a full day. She was tough as nails, but she was always well turned out. She had a huge, generous heart. She was one of those who would take in strangers to feed in hard times, even if she too was in the midst of those same hard times.

She could also really cook and bake. She was twice Washington Wheat Growers Association Baking Champion—the first time with basic white bread and the second time with something she called "King's Cake."

KICKIN' APPLE PIE ENCHILADAS

The cowgirl in the kitchen, Robin (who originally developed this recipe), says, "I revised the recipe because I found a better way to assemble them. Briefly putting them in a hot fry pan and flipping them makes them softer to work with for assembly. Then when you get them all done and the sauce in the pan, letting them sit also gives the sauce more time to integrate into the flour tortillas. An improvement!" You will agree!

2 tablespoons cornstarch
2 tablespoons water
2 cups apple juice or apple cider (sweetened)
5 medium tart apples (Jonagolds, Gravensteins, Gala, or Braeburn)
1 tablespoon lemon juice
1 chipotle pepper in adobo sauce (These come packed several to a 7-ounce can, but you need only 1 for a fiery kick.)
2 teaspoons butter
1/4 cup sugar
1 1/2 teaspoons cinnamon
10 (6-inch) flour tortillas
Additional sugar and cinnamon
Sharp cheddar cheese for serving
Vanilla ice cream for serving

1. Combine cornstarch and water in a small container and stir until dissolved. Pour the cornstarch mixture and apple juice or cider into a saucepan and heat to boiling over medium-high heat, stirring constantly. When the mixture begins to thicken, allow it to boil another 30 seconds, remove from heat, cover, and set aside.

2. Core, peel, and dice apples so that you have about 5 cups. Place apple cubes in cold water with the lemon juice to prevent them from browning.

3. Seed and chop the chipotle peppers.

4. In a sauté pan, melt the butter. Drain the apples and add them to the pan. Cook over medium heat until apples begin to soften, about 5 to 7 minutes. Then stir in the sugar, cinnamon, 1/2 teaspoon of chipotle pepper (less if you want it mild, more if you like it hot), and about 1/2 cup of the apple cider sauce. Cook another 3 to 5 minutes. Remove from heat and set aside for assembly of enchiladas.

5. Preheat the oven to 350°F. To assemble the enchiladas, soften each of the 10 flour tortillas by placing them in a hot frying pan for a minute or two, flipping to the other side, and leaving them in the pan for another minute. Take them out of the pan and stack them ready for filling.

6. Place about ¼ cup of the apple cube mixture in the middle of a prepared tortilla. Roll up and place in a well-buttered 7 x 11-inch baking dish, seam side down (an 8-inch square baking dish will also work, but will hold only about 8 enchiladas). Repeat with the remaining tortillas, setting them side by side in the pan.

7. Pour remaining apple cider sauce and any remaining apple mixture over the enchiladas. Let them rest for about 45 minutes before baking, or cover and place in the refrigerator overnight.

8. When ready to bake, sprinkle the enchiladas with additional sugar and cinnamon and bake for 25 to 30 minutes, or until the sauce is bubbling and the enchiladas are beginning to brown. Serve with sharp cheddar cheese and vanilla ice cream.

SERVES 4-8

ROBIN JOHNSON

LEATHER COOKIES

Jill says, "Every time I did a book signing with the original cookbook, The Cowgirl's Cookbook, I would take these cookies. Magic! Books sell like hot cakes when a prospective person eats this cookie. They are ridiculously easy to make (one bowl) and they keep well in an airtight container or frozen. Why the name? Because when they puff up in the oven and then droop down while cooling, they look like leather. They taste like heaven!"

3/4 cup shortening
1½ cups sugar, divided
1 egg, beaten well
1/4 cup molasses
1/2 teaspoon salt
2 teaspoons baking soda
1 teaspoon ground clove
1 teaspoon ground ginger
2 cups flour
1 cup raisins

1. Preheat the oven to 350°F. In a large bowl, cream the shortening, 1 cup of the sugar, and egg. Add molasses, salt, baking soda, spices, flour, and raisins.

2. Form dough into balls about the size of a walnut. Roll in the remaining sugar and place on an ungreased cookie sheet. Don't flatten—they do that all by themselves.

3. Bake the cookies for 8 to 10 minutes. Do not overbake. They should be chewy when cool. The resemblance of these good cookies to well-worn leather is startling. Don't let appearances fool you: Like good leather, you can rely on these.

MAKES ABOUT 4 DOZEN COOKIES

JILL STANFORD

LEMON SANDWICH CAKE WITH LEMON BUTTER CREAM AND JAM

Once in a while, a cowgirl has to come up with something pretty and special—as for a baby shower, a small wedding reception, or a summer picnic. This cake will wow the crowd. You can decorate it with edible wild flowers if you like. This is an old recipe and used to be called a "Victoria Sponge"—very "high tea!" Clean off your cowboy boots.

1. To make the cake, preheat the oven to 350°F and prepare 2 (9 x 9-inch) cake pans with grease and some flour sprinkled and then tapped out.

2. Combine the flour, baking powder, and salt. Whisk well until combined. Set aside.

3. In a large bowl, cream the butter and sugar well. Add the eggs, one at a time, stirring after each addition, and then add the vanilla and zest. Fold the flour mixture gently into the butter and egg mixture and add the milk so that it will be easier to pour (scoop) into the prepared cake pans.

4. Scoop/pour the batter into the prepared pans, trying to get them as even as possible. Bake on the center rack for about 25 minutes, or until a tooth-pick comes out clean when tested.

5. To make the butter cream, beat the butter and sugar together, add the vanilla and lemon zest, and beat until smooth.

6. Spread the butter cream on the bottom layer of the cake and then top with 1/2 cup of strawberry or raspberry jam. Arrange the top layer over the jam layer and sprinkle the entire cake with powdered sugar.

MAKES ONE CAKE

For the cake
11/4 cups self-rising flour
1 teaspoon baking powder
Pinch of salt
11/4 cups soft butter
11/4 cups granulated sugar
5 eggs
11/2 teaspoons vanilla
1 teaspoon lemon zest (or more if you want it really lemony)
3 tablespoons milk
1/2 cup strawberry or raspberry jam

For the Lemon Butter Cream
1/2 cup soft butter
1/2 cup powdered sugar
1/2 teaspoon vanilla
1/2 to 1 teaspoon lemon zest

MARY'S BIRTHDAY CAKE

Mary Rivers is a noted trick rider and trainer of trick horses and riders. She was featured in Jill's book, *Wild Women and Tricky Ladies*. As luck would have it, she was here in Central Oregon for her birthday, along with Cowgirl Patti Johnson, another "star" from that book. We wanted to make her a special cake—a cake like she is: sweet but not too sweet, a cake that stands apart from everything else and one you will never forget. We think we nailed it.

For the cake

10 tablespoons unsalted butter
1 cup stout beer, like Guinness (We used a chocolate stout.)
3/4 cup unsweetened cocoa powder
1½ cups sugar
1/2 cup dark brown sugar
3/4 cup sour cream
2 eggs
1 tablespoon vanilla extract
2 cups flour
2½ teaspoons baking soda
1/4 teaspoon salt
1 8-ounce jar of raspberry or strawberry jam for filling

1. To make the cake, preheat the oven to 350°F. Grease two 8- or 9-inch cake pans with butter and dust with flour.

2. In a large saucepan, mix together the butter and beer, cooking over medium-high heat until the butter has melted. Add the cocoa powder and sugars; whisk together. Take off the heat and let cool to room temperature.

3. In a separate bowl, whisk together the sour cream, eggs, and vanilla extract until well combined. Add to the butter mixture and whisk together well.

4. In a separate bowl, whisk together the flour, baking soda, and salt. Slowly whisk the flour mixture into the butter mixture until it all comes together.

5. Pour the batter into the cake pans and give the pan a few taps on the countertop to shake out any air pockets. Bake for 45 to 50 minutes. Let cool on a wire rack. Run a knife around the edges to separate the cakes from the pans and continue to cool on a wire rack, right side up.

6. To prepare the icing, cream the butter and cream cheese until fluffy. Add the vanilla extract and blend well.

7. Begin adding the confectioner's sugar, beating and stirring with each addition. You do not want any lumps. You can stop adding sugar when you know the icing will "hold" on top of the cake, that is, not dribble down the sides.

8. Place the first cake layer on a serving plate. For filling, you can use raspberry or strawberry jam. Use enough to fill the inner part of the cake. Put the second cake layer on top of the jam, and then frost it with the icing. Make swirls and "waves" on top.

MAKES ONE CAKE

For the icing
½ stick unsalted butter, softened
4 ounces cream cheese, softened
1 teaspoon vanilla extract
1½–2 cups confectioner's sugar

To be a cowgirl is more than just fluff and stuff. You have to do your share of the work, kill your own snakes, never complain, mount up even when you know you may get bucked off, and all the while being more of a lady at work than when you are at home.

—Georgie Sicking, National Cowgirl Hall of Fame honoree, 1989

PECAN CRESCENT MOON COOKIES

These are also known as Tea Cakes, Angel Wings, Snowballs (if you make them into balls, rolled in powdered sugar), and various other names. The bottom line is that they are easy to make and simply delicious.

2 cups all-purpose flour
2 cups finely chopped pecans
1/4 cup granulated sugar
1 cup (2 sticks) butter, softened
1 teaspoon vanilla
1 cup powdered sugar on a rimmed plate

1. Preheat the oven to 325°F. Combine all ingredients (except the powdered sugar) in bowl. Beat at low speed, scraping the bowl occasionally, until well mixed.

2. Shape the dough into 1-inch balls and then gently "bend" them into crescent shapes. Place the cookies 1 inch apart onto ungreased cookie sheets.

3. Bake 18 to 25 minutes, or until very lightly browned. Cool 5 minutes, then roll each cookie in powdered sugar. Cool on a rack and dust again with powdered sugar.

4. These freeze well. If you'd like to freeze them, put them in layers with waxed paper on top of each layer. Thaw them out and do the second dusting of powdered sugar.

MAKES 4-5 DOZEN COOKIES

RAW APPLE CAKE

No one seems to know where this recipe came from, but we're willing to bet it all started with a woman who had some apples, was sick of pies, and hated making frosting. What do you think? This is wonderful to take to a gathering, and we highly recommend ice cream or whipped cream as a garnish.

1. Preheat the oven to 325°F. In a large bowl, mix the apples, oil, sugar, eggs, nuts, raisins, vanilla, and vinegar.

2. In a separate bowl sift together the flour, cinnamon, baking soda, and salt.

3. Add the dry ingredients to the apple mixture. Pour into a greased 9 x 13-inch pan and bake for 1 hour.

SERVES 8-10

4 cups diced apples (Granny Smith, Gravenstein, or Gala are good.)
½ cup cooking oil
2 cups sugar
2 eggs, well beaten
1 cup chopped nuts
1 cup seedless raisins
2 teaspoons vanilla
1 tablespoon vinegar
2 cups flour
2 teaspoons cinnamon
2 teaspoons baking soda
1 teaspoon salt

ROBIN JOHNSON

AUNT PEARL'S RED VELVET CAKE WITH CREAM CHEESE ICING

Charmain Murray was asked to head up a heroic undertaking—a cookbook to benefit a horse camp with recipes submitted by members of horsecity.com, the largest site for horse enthusiasts on the World Wide Web. Needless to say, the recipes flooded her desk. Jill was asked to write the foreword to the cookbook. Somehow, with all she had to do, Charmain managed to get one of her favorite recipes in the book. She says, "This recipe came from my Aunt Pearl. You could bet if there was a church social or a family reunion, Aunt Pearl's Red Velvet Cake was there! She would be so proud to be in your book, too!"

For the cake
2 cups sugar
2 cups vegetable oil
2 eggs
2 teaspoons cocoa
1 teaspoon vanilla
1 (4-ounce) bottle red food coloring
1 teaspoon white vinegar
2½ cups self-rising cake flour
1 teaspoon salt
1 cup buttermilk
1 cup chopped nuts (for garnish)

1. To make the cake, preheat the oven to 350°F. Cream the sugar and oil until smooth. Add the eggs, one at a time, and blend well. Add the cocoa, vanilla, and red coloring. Last of all, add the vinegar. Mix well.

2. In a separate bowl, sift the flour and salt. Add this mixture alternately with the buttermilk to the wet ingredients until all are well blended.

3. Grease and flour three 8-inch cake pans. Divide the cake mixture evenly among the pans. Bake until a toothpick comes out clean from the center of each layer or when the edges pull away slightly from the sides of the pans, about 40 minutes.

4. Cool the cakes on a wire rack before frosting.

5. Meanwhile, prepare the icing. Cream the butter and cream cheese until smooth. Add the powdered sugar, 1/4 cup at a time, and beat until smooth. Add the vanilla and beat again.

6. When the cakes are cool, ice each layer with icing, including the top, and sprinkle the chopped nuts on top. Then ice the sides. Aunt Pearl says "ice" not frost—we like that.

SERVES 8

For the icing

1 stick (½ cup) unsalted butter, room temperature
1 (8-ounce) package cream cheese, room temperature
1 (1-pound) box powdered sugar
1 teaspoon vanilla

JORDYN KERR

SADDLEBAG PRALINES

Donna Higby, an Arizona cowgirl friend, says, "Deciding on a recipe to share with other cowgirls prompted me to think of one that could go in a saddlebag for a snack on the trail. This one packs nicely and can be a treat for your special horse. They are my go-to recipe to make for friends in the holiday season."

1 pound pecans (about 4 cups dry)
1 cup white sugar
1 teaspoon salt
1 teaspoon cinnamon
1 egg white

1. Preheat the oven to 275°F. Place the pecans in a bowl. In a separate bowl, mix the sugar, salt, and cinnamon.

2. Beat the egg white (just fluff it up a bit) and pour over the pecans. Stir to coat.

3. Sprinkle in the sugar mixture a little at a time, stirring to thoroughly coat the nuts.

ROBIN JOHNSON

4. Spread the pecans on a cookie sheet. Bake for 45 minutes, stirring every 15 minutes. Allow to cool . . . if you can wait!

MAKES APPROXIMATELY 1 POUND

Mapleine

When we made those amazing Better-Than-the-Bakery Bacon Maple Bars, found on page 44, we had never heard of Mapleine. By golly, there it was on the shelf of my local store, in the spice department. It did make all the difference in the bars, making them taste exactly like bakery maple bars. Curious about this unknown (to us) flavoring, we did a little research. Crescent brand's earliest incarnation was a spice business operated in a Seattle, Washington store in 1887, and their best-known product was Mapleine an imitation maple syrup. Introduced at the Puyallup, Washington Fair in 1908, it was an instant hit and became very popular during the Great Depression. It is said to have "made Seattle famous—and blessed among millions of lovers of maple sweets." Mapleine makes a nifty instant maple syrup, and it flavors cakes, breads, muffins, and cookies too. But we like this fudge best of all!

From the *Crescent Company Mapleine Dainties Cookbook*, 1913

Mapleine Fudge
2 cups granulated sugar
1 cup milk
1 piece (size of an egg) butter
1 heaping teaspoonful Mapleine

Cook about fifteen minutes.
Take off and beat hard until it grains, then pour in buttered plate.
Chopped nuts, figs, dates or coconut spread on the plate before pouring makes tasty variations.

The advertisement suggested that mothers should make lots of candy. Why? "Children crave sweets because their bodies need it." Mapleine Fudge is suggested to make sure the kiddies get their daily dose of sugar.
We're good with that!

SNOW ICE CREAM

When it blows and snows, here is a "free treat" to have with the hot cocoa!

8 cups clean and fresh snow
1 (14-ounce) can sweetened
   condensed milk
1 teaspoon vanilla extract

Place the snow into a large bowl. Pour condensed milk over it and add the vanilla. Mix gently to combine. Serve immediately in bowls. You also can add all or some of the following: shaved chocolate, 2 tablespoons chocolate syrup, crushed candy canes, nuts, or whatever suits your fancy!

We cowgirls have butted in on a so-called strictly man's game—and if to "play" on the hurricane deck on a sun-fishin', whirlly-giggin', rearin'-up, fallin'-over-backward, squallin', bitin', strikin', buckin', roman-nosed cayuse ain't a he-man's game, there never will be one—still, as I say, we cowgirls that like the game well enough to play it should play it just like the cowboys do. Why, I'd feel insulted . . . if I was told to tie my stirrups down!

—Bonnie McCarroll

TAMARACK TEA CAKES

For many girls aged nine to seventeen, a four-week session at Camp Tamarack, on the shores of Dark Lake in Central Oregon, was the turning point in their lives. Not only did they get to ride horseback through the fragrant pines all day long, swim and canoe in and on the crystal-clear waters of Dark Lake, and sleep under tents on starry nights following the evening campfire and "Taps" played by a bugler at the foot of the flagpole each and every night, but they also came under the spell of the owner, founder, and director, Donna Gill.

From the beginning, the program was innovative. Activities took place at all times. The emphasis was on horseback riding, swimming, boating, crafts, and the indefinable quality of being a "good scout," Donna's highest praise.

Donna instilled in the Tamarackers a set of standards and taught them to accept responsibility. Her rule was that no girl should ever do anything that would endanger another person or cause unhappiness. At the end of each session, July and August, parents were invited for a special display of mounted drills, swimming and diving exhibitions, archery, and crafts. A gala luncheon was served with the traditional Tamarack Tea Cakes for dessert.

Donna died in 1983. But her spirit lives on in women who still strive to be "good scouts."

1. Preheat the oven to 350°F. Using a wooden spoon, cream the butter and powdered sugar in a large bowl until well blended. Add the vanilla and mix again. Add the flour and the pecans and mix well.

2. Roll the dough into balls about the size of a Ping-Pong ball. Place these on an ungreased cookie sheet and bake until golden, about 8 minutes. Watch that they don't burn.

3. Roll the warm tea cakes in powdered sugar and place on waxed paper to cool and dry.

MAKES ABOUT 36 TEA CAKES

1 cup soft butter
6 tablespoons
   powdered sugar
1 teaspoon vanilla
2 cups cake flour
1 cup chopped
   pecans
Powdered sugar for
   rolling

COWGIRL PENDLETON WHISKY FUDGE

This is fudge with a definite kick! It makes a great gift, if you can bear to share any of it, that is!

19 ounces bittersweet
chocolate, chopped well
1 (14-ounce) can sweetened
condensed milk
⅓ cup Pendleton Whisky
½ cup chopped walnuts
(optional)

1. Lightly grease a 9 x 9-inch pan.

2. Put the chopped chocolate and condensed milk in a medium saucepan and heat, stirring, over medium-low heat until the chocolate is almost melted.

3. Remove mixture from heat and add the whisky. Stir until very smooth. Add the walnuts if you like a nutty fudge.

4. Spread the fudge evenly in the prepared pan. Cover and refrigerate until firm. Cut in squares.

5. Lick the spoon and the pan.

MAKES ABOUT 16 SQUARES

CAMPING AND CAST IRON

ANY BERRY DUTCH OVEN COBBLER

If you are lucky enough to go out into the wilderness, this is a dessert you won't regret taking along. It calls for only three ingredients, so it was easy to pack in the pack saddles when we took a pack trip to the Eagle Cap Wilderness in Oregon's Wallowa Mountains. Our camp cook shared this with us, and now we are sharing it with you. We wish we were going to be with you to enjoy it!

You will need a heavy, 6-quart Dutch oven with a lid that has a lip. Why? So you can shovel the hot coals on top to make it cook.

1 box white cake mix
2 cups any canned berry pie filling (A mix of berries will do nicely—blueberries travel well.)
1 cup sugar
1 (12-ounce) can lemon-flavored soda

1. Empty the cake mix into a gallon-size ziplock bag. Close securely.

2. Put the berries, washed (and hulled if need be), in another ziplock bag along with the sugar; close securely.

3. Don't worry about the soda until you are going to open it—when you do, point it away from yourself and others, because it will be pretty fizzed up.

4. Start a good campfire and allow the wood to burn down to hot, glowing coals. Empty the berries into the Dutch oven.

5. Pour the soda over the cake mix in its bag and mix it together. It will be lumpy, but no matter.

IT'S PRETTY SMART TO PUT ALL YOUR INGREDIENTS INTO ANOTHER ZIPLOCK BAG BIG ENOUGH TO HOLD ALL THREE. CLOSED SECURELY, OF COURSE!

6. Pour the cake mix over the berries and then lower the Dutch oven into your hot coals. Shovel 20 coals on top (you don't have to be picky about this—just enough to cover the lid will do) and leave the rest on the bottom.

7. Bake until the cake is golden brown, about 30 minutes.

8. Scrape off the top coals and lift up the Dutch oven from the bed of coals. Remove the lid to let it cool.

9. If you packed an 8-ounce can of evaporated milk for your campfire coffee in the morning, and it is cooling in the mountain stream or lake, so much the better! Pour some over this cobbler.

SERVES 6 HUNGRY PACKERS

ROBIN JOHNSON

CAMPFIRE COFFEE

Joie Smith lived high up on the flanks of Mount Hood in a log cabin. Joie loved nothing more than camping with her horses and her friends. Three meals a day cooked over a roaring campfire was part of the magic, and we were fortunate indeed to be a part of it. The rest of the time was spent riding the trails. You become instantly awake on cold mountain mornings with Joie's coffee, done in a battered old graniteware pot, blackened by many fires. "Always bury the grounds under a tree," Joie always admonished us.

Fresh and cold water
2 heaping tablespoons ground coffee per person
1 tablespoon salt
1 eggshell, broken into medium-size pieces

ROBIN L. GREEN

1. Pour the water into the coffee pot, preferably one made of graniteware, filling nearly to the brim.

2. Put the pot over the fire and add the coffee.

3. Add the salt.

4. When the coffee starts to boil, remove the pot from the fire and put the eggshell pieces in. The shells will cause the coffee grounds to settle to the bottom.

5. Keep the coffee warm beside the fire, but don't allow it to boil again.

6. Bury the grounds under a tree later.

SERVES 4

I've been around, believe me, and nothing compares to the great outdoors.

—Jane Westlund, Forest Service Packer, 1928–1935

CAST-IRON CORNMEAL FLAPJACKS

What is more fun that going out camping on an early fall day? The leaves are turning, and it is time for breakfast. Try these in your cast-iron skillet. This camping-out breakfast was done right in Robin's backyard. Brilliant idea!

1. In a large bowl, mix the cornmeal with the baking mix, then add the eggs and milk. Let this sit for 30 minutes in the refrigerator to soften the cornmeal. If the batter is too thick to pour for pancakes, add more milk until it is the consistency you like. If you want, add the blueberries and/or the bacon bits at this point.

2. Heat a cast-iron skillet until it is hot (test by throwing a few water drops on the skillet; when they sizzle, it is ready!) Pour silver dollar–size rounds on the skillet, and when they start to bubble, carefully turn them over to continue to cook until both sides are golden brown.

3. Enjoy with real maple syrup and more bacon!

SERVES 4-6

½ cup cornmeal
1½ cups prepared baking mix
2 eggs
1 cup milk
½ cup fresh blueberries and/
    or cooked, crispy bacon
    bits (both are optional)
Maple syrup for serving

ROBIN JOHNSON

CAST-IRON ROASTY CHICKIE

Robin says, "I do this about once a week; my husband Jim and I love it. I did it last night and the cast iron does a great job! Enjoy cold chickie tonight with a salad. Then you can use the baked bones and extra meat to make stock and do chicken noodle soup."

½ cup rough-cut carrots (1-inch pieces)
½ cup rough-cut celery (1-inch pieces)
½ cup rough-cut onion (1-inch pieces)
1 lemon
1 (5- to 6-pound) whole roasting chicken
¼ cup olive oil
Kosher salt and freshly ground pepper to taste
1 tablespoon seasoned salt

1. Preheat the oven to 375°F. Lightly oil a 4- or 5-quart cast-iron Dutch oven. (Actually any Dutch oven this size will do!)

2. Cut carrots, celery, and onion. Mix them together and place in the bottom of the oiled Dutch oven. Wash the lemon, pierce the skin in several places, and set aside.

3. Unwrap the chicken, remove the giblets from the cavity, and pat dry with a paper towel. Place the bird, breast side up, on top of the cut vegetables in the Dutch oven. Insert the pierced lemon in the large cavity. You can truss the legs and wings or not; it's your choice. A rubber band works well if you only want to truss the legs.

4. Pour the olive oil on the bird and rub with your hands to evenly distribute the oil. Generously salt and pepper the bird and then sprinkle the seasoned salt on top.

5. Place the bird, uncovered, in the preheated oven and roast for 1½ to 2 hours, or until a thermometer (meat or insta-read) measures 165°F to 170°F in the thickest part of the thigh, being careful not to touch the bone.

6. When it's done, lift the bird out of the Dutch oven and place on a platter. Let the bird rest before carving, about 30 minutes.

7. You can strain the juices in the bottom of the Dutch oven and make gravy, or use the strained juices to moisten the chicken while serving.

SERVES 4

CHICKEN NOODLE IN A POT

This is from Jean Brown, an experienced backcountry packer who travels on her mule with a string of more mules behind her, in Idaho's rugged wild and scenic Middle Fork of the Salmon River. Her expertise is amazing.

1 canned whole chicken, undrained
1 (12-ounce) bag egg noodles
8 cups water
2 tablespoons dehydrated onion
2 tablespoons dehydrated celery
1 bay leaf
Salt (or garlic salt) and pepper to taste

Put all the ingredients in your Dutch oven.

SERVES 8 HUNGRY CAMPERS

Jean says: "For a 9 x 6-inch Dutch oven (this is the best size to use because it is versatile), dig an 18 x 12-inch-deep hole next to your fire pit. Shovel about 6 inches of hot coals on the bottom of the hole you've dug and set the Dutch oven, with your meal prepared in it, on top. Put more hot coals around the sides and 4 inches of coals on the top. Now cover it all up with dirt. (You can also lay foil on top of the coals to hold in the heat.) Now saddle up and ride all day and when you come back, dinner is ready."

CHEESY CORN BREAD CASSEROLE

Cowgirl Fran Rattay and her trusty trailer, "Kelly Sue," are members of Sisters on the Fly, a group of women who love nothing better than to hitch up and hit the road. When they get there, they like to cook outdoors. Fran says this recipe "never has any leftovers."

1. Melt the butter in a Dutch oven and sauté the onion until it is transparent. Then mix in all the other ingredients.

2. To bake, place 8 to 10 coals underneath the Dutch oven, and 16 resting on top. Cook for 50 to 60 minutes.

3. Remove from the coals and let it "set" for 10 minutes before serving.

SERVES 6

½ cup (1 stick) butter

½ medium onion, chopped

1 (8.5-ounce) box prepared corn bread mix

1 egg

1 cup grated sharp cheddar cheese

1 cup grated pepper jack cheese

1 (4-ounce) can fire-roasted chopped chiles

1 (15-ounce) can cream-style corn

1 (15-ounce) can whole-kernel corn, drained

Just because you are following a well-marked trail don't mean whoever made it knew where they were going.

—Unknown

DUTCH OVEN MEAT LOAF

Jennifer Denison is the senior editor and Cowboy Culture editor for *Western Horseman* magazine. When sharing this recipe with us, she said, "Growing up, both of my parents worked, so one of my chores was to start dinner each night when I got home from school. Meat loaf was a hearty favorite that produced leftovers, so I made it frequently and became known for my meat loaf recipe. Through the years, I have modified it. The past year, I started cooking in Dutch ovens over the fire and found my meat loaf recipe worked well in Dutch ovens. I hosted a Dutch-oven party this fall, and people enjoyed learning about the traditional cooking method, and the meat loaf was a huge hit!"

¾ cup milk

1 egg

2 cups chopped or torn corn
    tortillas

1 teaspoon salt

1 teaspoon pepper

½ teaspoon oregano

½ teaspoon dried basil

½ teaspoon chopped garlic

1 small onion, minced

1 green bell pepper, minced

2 tablespoons
    Worcestershire sauce,
    divided

1 pound lean ground beef, elk,
    or venison

1 pound Italian sausage

1 cup catsup

1 tablespoon brown sugar

1. Combine the milk, egg, tortilla pieces, spices, garlic, onion, bell pepper, 1 tablespoon Worcestershire sauce, and meat in a large bowl and mix well with your hands. Shape into a loaf and place into a 12-inch Dutch oven that has been coated with cooking spray or olive oil.

2. Place Dutch oven over medium-hot coals. Add coals to the top of the Dutch oven and cook for an hour or so, or until done throughout.

3. Combine catsup, brown sugar, and remaining 1 tablespoon Worcestershire sauce in a pan and bring to a boil. Pour over meat loaf and bake 10 additional minutes.

SERVES 6

ROBIN JOHNSON

Cast Iron Tips

When you buy a cast-iron skillet, or a Dutch oven, or anything else made of cast iron, you are buying an item that will serve you and your family well. It is also an item that can be passed onto the next generation if you take proper care of it.

Robin used the cast-iron Dutch oven that belonged to our mother for the recipes in this book. She will pass it on to her daughter.

The more you use your cast iron, the better, because you will be taking care of it. Here are some other tips.

- Clean the cast iron after every use, using only warm water while the iron is still warm. We repeat: use only warm water. No. Soap. Never, ever, pinky-swear, put your cast-iron in the dishwasher!

- Buy a coarse bristled brush to clean the bits of food left in the cast iron.

- Dry the cast iron with paper towels and then give it a light coating of vegetable oil. This is "seasoning" your cast iron. Think of it like moisturizer for your skin. It pays off in the long run!

- When you store your cast iron, put a paper towel between the lid and the pot to create airflow and avoid rust. You can also put a little dry rice on the bottom to absorb any moisture.

- If you find a piece of cast-iron at a garage sale, and it is really cheap because it is rusty, buy it and then do this: Rub it with steel wool. Really rub it well! Then wash it with warm water and, just this once, a mild dish soap. Dry it well! Then rub it with vegetable oil—inside, outside, on the handle, everywhere. Then wipe away the excess. Finally, bake the iron in a 400°F oven for about an hour. Place it, upside down, on the lowest rack that has been lined with foil. You may have to repeat the oiling and baking several times to get the desired glossy nonstick sheen so loved by cast iron fans.

SMOKEY'S DUTCH OVEN (OR SLOW COOKER) BEANS

Jill met Sue Tebow outside of Ellensburg at a cowgirl gathering put on by her friend, photographer Robin L. Green. Sue told her about her ranch and mentioned that during branding one of the asked-for and favorite recipes was this amazing bean recipe from Smokey Reich, better known as Grandpa Smokey. He is a self-taught Dutch-oven cooker who has his own little trailer that he pulls behind his pickup with his "kitchen" and loves to cook for people. "He cooks for twenty-five to thirty people for our branding," Sue said. I shared this with Robin, who cooked it and loved it!

If you don't have a Dutch oven handy, use your slow cooker. The results are just as good, and there are no bawling calves. And if you are not planning on feeding a branding crew, by all means, cut this recipe in half.

3-4 tart apples, peeled and cut into chunks
1 stick butter
1 cup brown sugar
1 cup white sugar
½ cup dark molasses
1 tablespoon cinnamon
2 (15-ounce) cans pinto beans
2 (15-ounce) cans red beans
2 (15-ounce) cans white navy beans
2 (15-ounce) cans black beans

1. Saute the apples in the butter until soft. Then add the brown sugar, white sugar, molasses, and cinnamon. Cook and stir this mixture until the sugars have dissolved.

2. Add the beans, draining all the cans first. Stir well and simmer at least 2 hours over a slow fire if you are using a Dutch oven, with the lid on, and stirring now and then. If you are using a slow cooker, put the lid on and cook on low for 6 hours.

SERVES 8

WE ALL AGREED THAT A NICE ADDITION WOULD BE A HAM BONE OR HAM HOCKS, OR A GOOD SAUSAGE, LIKE KIELBASA, CUT INTO ROUNDS.

STREAMSIDE BROOK TROUT

Rivers, lakes, and streams abound out in the West. Trout lurk in the cold waters, and you might see Sally Hutchins lurking on the bank with a rod and reel in her hands. Tied to a tree or shrub nearby is her horse and only companion on these fishing trips, Buster. In his saddlebags, Buster carries a cast-iron skillet, a tin plate and fork, some flour in a large, zipped-tight plastic bag, and a little bacon fat in a discarded "snoose" can. He waits patiently for Sally to catch her limit.

Then Sally builds a little fire; cleans and cooks her catch; tosses it in the flour in the bag; heats the bacon fat in the skillet until it starts smoking; fries the fish; eats it; washes the pan, plate, and fork; puts the fire out—twice for good measure; repacks the saddlebags; mounts Buster; and rides home to her little cabin. It has been a perfect day for Sally. Buster, too.

2 fresh trout
4 tablespoons bacon fat
    wrapped in aluminum foil
    or plastic wrap
2 tablespoons flour in a
    plastic bag

1. Clean the trout, leaving on the tails, but cut off the heads; they take up too much room in the skillet.

2. Get the fire going hot, put the skillet over the coals, and melt the bacon fat. Dredge the trout in the flour right in the bag, then lay them in the sizzling fat. Brown one side, about 3 minutes. Pick them up by the tail and turn them over to brown the other side.

3. Use the bag for the bones and take them with you when you leave. Make sure your fire is out by dousing it with water, then kicking dirt over the wet coals. Use the gravel from the stream or lake to clean your frying pan.

SERVES 2, OR 1 HUNGRY COWGIRL

COWGIRLS IN THE KITCHEN

ALL THINGS COWGIRL—
A SHORT LIST OF SOURCES

We are pleased to include this list of places to visit from the comfort of your computer that will enrich your knowledge of all things Cowgirl.

Western Horseman magazine
http://www.westernhorseman.com/subscribe
We were so pleased that Jennifer Dennison, the senior editor of *Western Horseman* magazine agreed to contribute a few recipes! Jennifer is a busy gal, traveling hither and yon to find the very best of the West for her articles about everything under the sun to be found in the West. She's dab hand with a cook-pot too. The magazine is a wealth of Western treasures each month, from horsemanship to horse care, cowboy and cowgirl culture, and a lot more. If you don't already subscribe, then do it now.

Cast Iron Cooking
http://www.realsimple.com/food-recipes/cooking-tips-techniques/preparation/cleaning-seasoning-cast-iron-skillet
The Internet is a wealth of information on nearly every subject you can dream up. If you just got your very first cast-iron skillet and can't figure out what the next step is, the website we have listed is very clear and helpful on the "care and feeding of cast iron." Some say they won't cook on or in anything else. For a meal around the campfire, there is nothing better.

Slow Cooking
Just "Google" any recipe you want with the words "slow cooker," and dinner (or breakfast or lunch) will be ready as soon as you decide which recipe appeals to you! There are a wide variety of sizes and brands available. We believe that the one that fits your budget and size of your family will be the "right" one. While we think the "warm" option is handy, it is not absolutely necessary.

Twist N Ties
http://www.twistnties.com
Cindy Forbes, up in Ronan, Montana, makes the most beautiful "wild rags" in pure silk as well as polyester.

What's a "wild rag"? It is, along with boots, Wranglers, and a hat, the most useful piece of apparel a cowgirl or a cowboy can own. It keeps your neck warm in the winter and adds a touch of color on a gray winter day. It keeps you cool in the summer and, worn "bandit-style," keeps the dust out of your nose and mouth if you are riding drag behind a whole lot of steers headed down the trail. Cindy provided you with the Better-Than-the-Bakery Bacon Maple Bars, by the way. In addition to her handmade scarves, she makes rope and antler baskets. Go and stop by for a visit, why don't you?

KitchenAid
http://www.kitchenaid.com/countertop-appliances/stand-mixers/
Did you wonder about all those cookies and other doughs in the book? How did we do that? Creaming the butter and sugar and adding flour, and so on? We used our trusty stand mixers from KitchenAid, and if you don't already have one, we urge you to get one. They make all the dough mixing a breeze! It's one thing to be tough as nails and ride bucking broncos, but when it comes to mixing up a batch of Leather Cookies? Go the easy route, like we did. Life is too short to have to work that hard these days!

Cowfolks Care
http://cowfolkscare.com/home.html
We certainly like and support this fine institution run by cowgirls that provides financial assistance to folks who find themselves in need due to unforeseen hardships in the agricultural and ranching community. Monies are raised as assistance through online auctions of donated items from all the members on Facebook. The chosen recipients have been varied, from rodeo wrecks to sick babies.

Hamley & Company
Pendleton, Oregon
http://www.hamleyco.com
We have been asked, several times, what we consider to be "the" best place to shop for Western tack and apparel. We would have to say, hands-down, it is this iconic store that takes up an entire city block in the rodeo-based town of Pendleton, Oregon, home of the world-famous Pendleton Round-Up. Let 'Er Buck! Saddles and tack, giftware, art, books, men's and women's clothing, boots, jewelry, and accessories—Hamley's has it all, and only the best will do. When you get tired of shopping, slip into a booth at the next-door Hamley Steakhouse & Barbecue, where they will bring you a shot of Pendleton Whisky (the cowgirls' choice) while you ponder the lengthy menu. We know that there are many fine Western stores throughout the United States, but, as Oregonians, we are justifiably proud of this fine establishment that opened its doors to cowboys and cowgirls in 1905.

Bennett Custom Spurs
Goldendale, Oregon
Pete Bennett began building spurs after he retired from cowboy work. For a long time Pete had thought about wanting to build spurs. Before he started on building spurs, he researched cowboy spurs deeply and got a clear idea of what type of spurs he'd want to make. He didn't want to work doing fancy engraving on silver. His eye and mind were drawn to the early, rustic, and primitive spurs that he saw in history books. Pete knew he wanted his spurs to look old, vintage, and used. Over the last ten years, he has not really veered from his early vision. He will make spurs to a customer's request and design. You can order your spurs in polished steel (not chrome, not stainless), or with a dark gray tint or a brown/rust tint. You can select from spurs he has in stock or he can start from scratch to build just the spurs you've been dreaming of, or the spurs you will be proud to give to a loved one. Send Pete a private message by emailing him at virginiabennett@embarqmail.com

Music of the Real West
www.rangeradio.com
While you are whipping up something delicious from this book, tune into this traditional, roots-based classic country music station. All your Western artists are here, just waiting for you to sing along, twenty-four hours a day.

Happy trails to you! And happy cooking!

Jill and Robin

INDEX